TOMAS POLAK
WITH JIRI RAJLICH & PAVEL VA

C000041305

Colour artwork : Malcolm Laird

Layout & project design : Phil Listemann

Copyright © Tomas Polak and Phil Listemann 2006

ISBN 2-9526381-1-X

Edited by Phil H. Listemann

philedition@wanadoo.fr

Printed in France by
GRAPHIC SUD
BP44 - ZAC de Rigoulet
47552 Boé Cedex, France
Tél : (33).5.53.48.20.30 - Fax : (33).5.53.48.20.35
igs@wanadoo.fr

ACKNOWLEDGEMENTS

Jim Grant, M.J. Ingham, Vaclav Kolesa, Malcolm Laird, Chris Shores, Jan Rail, Paul Sortehaug, Ray Sturtivant, Andy Thomas.

GLOSSARY OF TERMS

AACU : Anti-Aircraft Cooperation Unit
ADF : Aircraft Delivery Flight
ADGB : Air Defense of Great Britain
ADU : Aircraft Delivery Unit
AFC : Air Force Cross
AFDU : Air Fighting Development Unit
AGS : Advanced Gunnery School
ALG : Advanced Landing Ground
APC : Armament Practice Camp
CIG : Czechoslovak Inspectorate General
Cz : Czech
(CZ) : Czechoslovak serving in the RAF
CzAF : Czechoslovakian Air Force
DFC : Distinguished Flying Cross

DFM : Disting
DSO : Distinguished Service Order
EC : *Ecole de Chasse* (French), Fighter School
EFTS : Elementary Flying Training Unit
ELD : *Escadrille Légère de Défense* (French), Fighter Flight
Eva : Evaded
FAF : French Air Force
FE : Far East
FIS : Flying Instructors School
F/L : Flight Lieutenant
FLS : Fighter Leaders School
F/O : Flying Officer
FPP : Ferrey Pilots Pool
F/Sgt : Flight Sergeant
FTS : Flying Training School
GBA : *Groupe de Bombardement et d'Attaque* (French), Strike Squadron
GC : *Groupe de Chasse* (French), Fighter Squadron
GCS : Group Communications Squadron
GSU : Group Support Unit
HQ : Headquarters
HQFC : Headquarters Fighter Command
LAC : Leading Aircraftman
LG : London Gazette
MBE : Member of British Empire
ME : Middle East
MU : Maintenance Unit
(NZ)/RAF : New Zealander serving in the RAF
ORB : Operational Record Book
OTU : Operational Training Unit
(P)AFU : (Pilots) Advanced Flying Unit
PDC : Personnel Despatch Centre
PDRC : Personnel Despatch and Reception Centre
PAF : Polish Air Force
P/O : Pilot Officer
PoW : Prisoner of War
R&SU : Repair and Salvage Unit
SFTS : Service Flying Training School
Sgt : Sergeant
S/L : Squadron Leader
S of AC : School of Army Cooperation
Sqn : Squadron
SS : Signals School
SSC : Short Service Commission
RAF : Royal Air Force
W/C : Wing Commander
W/O : Warrant Officer

In the middle of the Battle of Britain, the pilots of No.310 Squadron are posing for the photographer at Duxford on 7th September 1940.
Standing, left to right :P/O S. Janouch, Sgt J. Vopalecky, Sgt R. Puda, Sgt K. Seda, Sgt B. Fürst, Sgt R. Zima.
Seated, left to right : P/O V. Göth, F/L J. Maly (Czech A Flight commander), F/L G.L. Sinclair (A Flight commander), F/O J.E. Boulton, F/L J. Jefferies (B Flight commander), P/O S. Zimprich, Sgt J. Kaucky, F/L F. Rypl (Czech B Flight commander), P/O E. Fechtner and P/O V. Bergman (IWM CH1299)

MAIN EQUIPMENT 1940-1945			
HURRICANE I	07.40 - 03.41	SPITFIRE VI	07.43 - 09.43
HURRICANE II	03.41 - 12.41	SPITFIRE IX	01.44 - 07.44
SPITFIRE II	10.41 - 12.41	SPITFIRE V	07.44 - 08.44
SPITFIRE V	11.41 - 02.44	SPITFIRE IX	08.44 - 10.45

In the summer of 1940 Great Britain alone remained in the fight against Nazi´s Third Reich. In this serious situation it was decided to accept into the Royal Air Force thousands of foreigners who had fled to Great Britain. They were willing to fight for the King especially against the Germans. As early as July 1940, the Royal Air Force began to form new squadrons manned by Continental Europeans. Those units received a number in the 300 series. The Dutch, Poles and Czechoslovaks were the first three nationalities which raised new units under RAF command followed by France, Norway, Belgium, Greece and Yugoslavia.

The first Czechoslovak squadron was created at Duxford on 10th July 1940 as No.310 (Czechoslovak) Squadron and on the same day two British pilots, Flight Lieutenants J. Jefferies and G. Sinclair arrived to become the first two flight commanders. Two days

later 24 fighter pilots of the pre-war Czechoslovakian Air Force arrived and these were joined by another 9 on the following day. The first officers were Alexander Hess, Jan Ambruz, Vaclav Bergman, Emil Fechtner, Vilem Göth, Jaroslav Himr, Frantisek Hradil Rudolf Holecek, Vladislav Chocholin, Svatopluk Janouch, Frantisek Kordula, Miloslav Kredba, Jaroslav Maly, Antonin Navratil, Rudolf Rohacek, Frantisek Rypl, Jaroslav Sterbacek, Karel Vykoukal, Vladimir Zaoral and Stanislav Zimprich. The N.C.O.s were Josef Hubacek, Vaclav Jicha, Josef Kubak, Miroslav Kopecky, Frantisek Marek, Eduard Prchal, Jindrich Postolka, Josef Vopalecky, Rudolf Zima. Some of these had gained combat experience during their service with the French Air Force. By the 17th July an additional 20 pilots and ground personnel arrived and the following day the squadron's first CO,

---

SERIALS OF HURRICANE I IN USE ON 23RD AUGUST 1940.

L : 1596
P : 3056, 3142, 3143, 3148, 3156, 3157, 3159, 3887, 3888, 3889, 3960, 8809, 8811, 8814
R : 4084, 4085, 4087, 4089

Total : 19

Squadron Leader George D.M. Blackwood arrived to take command. Their first aircraft, four brand new Hawker Hurricane Mk.Is were delivered that same day. Although Czechoslovaks had good officers capable of leading the unit dual command was thought to be necessary because of their lack of experience with British procedures. In accordance with this decision Squadron Leader Alexander Hess was posted as second in command of the unit while Flight Lieutenants Jaroslav Maly and Frantisek Rypl were made deputy Flight Commanders to Flight Lieutenants G. L. Sinclair and J. Jefferies.

INTO THE BATTLE

Despite the large number of pilots in the unit none were in fact combat ready for a number of reasons. The first was that none had been checked out on the Hurricane, some had been retrained by the French had used their procedures but all pilots had to be taught British procedures. A refresher course was then scheduled for all pilots which would take care of the latter problem. The first groups left for Cosford on the 19th July and within three days no less that 25 pilots were posted out of the Squadron. The other problem was their poor knowledge of the English language and, during July and August, three lessons per week were held to improve the level of each pilot. By 25th July, the squadron had 16 Hurricanes and pilots were flying every day. The intensive training caused some minor accidents with Pilot Officer E. Fechtner damaging an aircraft on 1st August while landing and on 15th August Pilot Officer E. Fechtner and Pilot Officer A. Navratil collided during a mock dogfight, however both pilots

To ease the integration of the Czechoslovaks into the RAF, a number of British pilots were posted to No.310 Squadron, at Duxford, during the Summer of 1940. Amongst these were Squadron Leader G.D.M. Blackwood, Flying Officer J.E. Boulton, Flight Lieutenant J. Jefferies, and Flight Lieutnant G.L. Sinclair. They all played a major role during the first weeks of the squadron's existence. (www.ww2images.com)

From left to right, the prewar Czechoslovak Air Force's Regiment's badges, 1st to 6th.

WHAT THEY DID BEFORE JOINING THE RAF

When World War II broke out in September 1939, Czechoslovakia had already ceased to exist. The country which had been created at the end of WWI from former Austro-Hungarian territories had built up strong armed forces in the years between the wars. It also had a competitive aeronautical industry which allowed it to be almost self-sufficient. By the time of the Munich Crisis the Czechoslovakian Air Force (CzAF) consisted of six Air Regiments, one fighter (4th), three mixed fighter/reconnaissance (1st, 2nd, 3rd), and two bombers (5th and 6th). A total of more than 1,500 aircraft, about 830 of them being first-line types including more than 320 fighters were available to the Allied cause. Its pilots and aircrew were well trained and motivated. After September 1938 when French and Britsih politicians sold out to Germany, this Air Force was gradually disbanded. The final chapter in Czechoslovakia's short history took place in March 1939 when the country was split into two parts. Bohemia-Moravia which was made a German protectorate, and Slovakia, officially independent from the Germans, but with strong political and military links.

Soldiers, pilots and other aircrew were demobilised and many chose to escape from their country and find asylum in Poland, where some remained, or France, the preferred choice for most of them. By September 1939 nearly 500 of them had joined the French forces, serving at first in the French Foreign Legion for diplomatic reasons as France and Germany were not yet at war. With the oubreak of war the French were happy to find additional well-trained pilots in their midst and they were transferred to the *Armée de l'Air* (French Air Force - FAF) in October 1939. The first pilots were ready for active service as early as December 1939 but were scattered throughout French fighter units (*Groupe de Chasse* - GC), though a few found their way to bomber or reconnaissance units. As other Czechoslovak airmen arrived they were sent to the Czech Depot at Agde near the Mediterranean coast for future allocation to units. Plans to create separate Czechoslovakian units were in hand but these did not come to fruition. Nevertheless the Czechs performed well, and were much appreciated by the French. About 157 confirmed or probable victories were claimed by Czechoslovak pilots, although a number of these would have been classified as "shared" under the British system of calculating kills. Some pilots like Alois Vasatko, with 15 victories, and Frantisek Perina with 14 were amongst the top aces in the French Air Force during the Phoney war and the battle of France. These scores were not achieved without cost, 28 airmen were killed while serving with the French. With the end of the Battle of France, the Czechoslovaks withdrew to Great Britain, the last European country still fighting against Nazi Germany. The Czechoslovaks had not yet been defeated. By 15th August 1940 more than 900 former CzAF personnel had reached Great Britain and this total rose to nearly 1,300 by the end of 1940. These men were the nucleus of four Czech units, Nos.310, 312 and 313 fighter Squadrons, and No.311 bomber Squadron. One night fighter flight was raised as part of No.68 Squadron.

They were to fight well for a foreign King and country and some, at least, survived to return to their own liberated country.

Czech front-line pilots killed serving with the French

Sgt Josef BENDL	†07.06.40	GC I/6	Sgt Josef KOSNAR	†05.06.40	GC III/7
Lt Jindrich BERAN (1)	†12.05.40	GC III/3	Sgt Jan KRAKORA	†23.04.40	GC I/1
Lt Frantisek BIEBERLE (1)	†25.05.40	GC I/6	Lt Jiri KRAL (1)	†08.06.40	GC I/1
S/Lt Josef DEKASTELLO (1)	†03.06.40	GC I/8	Sgt Antonin KRALIK (1)	†27.05.40	GC I/8
Lt Frantisek DYMA	†21.05.40	GC III/7	Lt Antonin MIKOLASEK (2)	†25.05.40	GC II/3
Lt Jaroslav GLEICH (2)	†13.06.40	GC II/3	S/Chef Emil MORAVEK	†15.06.40	GC I/5
Cap Timoteus HAMSIK (1)	†14.05.40	GC I/5	S/Chef Josef NOVAK	†02.06.40	GC III/3
Adj Josef HRANICKA (1)	†03.06.40	GC I/6	Sgt Stanislav POPELKA (1)	†03.06.40	GC I/6
Lt Otakar KOREC	†05.06.40	GC I/3	Sgt Vladimir VASEK	†02.01.40	GC I/5

Furthermore, other Czech airmen were killed, at CIC (*Centre d'Instruction à la Chasse* - Fighter OTU) :

Sol. Frantisek BARTON (06.10.39), Lt Vladimir KUCERA (14.05.40), Sgt Miloslav RAJTR (11.01.40)

or at CIB (*Centre d'Instruction au Bombardement* - Bomber OTU) :

Sol. Jaroslav KRIZEK (15.11.39), Cap Jaroslav Novak (15.12.39) and Cpl Jaroslav STOKLASA (04.03.40) or for other causes, Capt Frantisek NOVAK (27.04.40, illness), Capt Jan CERNY (11.05.40, air raid), and Sgt Frantisek MASEK (18.06.40, bomber pilot, accident), as well Cpl Zdenech EICHELMAN, mechanic (29.04.40).

In brackets, the number of victories claimed with the French.

Four types of French fighters were flown by the Czechoslovaks during the 1939-1940 campaign.

From the top, the Morane Saulnier MS-406, which equipped most of the French fighter units at the outbreak of war. This aircraft had a lot of shortcomings, it was almost totally obsolete, it could not match the Bf 109E and they were being phased out of service in 1940.

The Bloch family (the MB 151 and 152) began to be issued to squadrons at the end of 1939. Their best features were a good armament, with two 20 mm cannons and two machine-guns installed in the MB 152, and their ability to absorb a lot of battle damage. Otherwise they were generally outclassed by the Bf 109E.

The Dewoitine 520 was put into service in March 1940 and was the best French fighter at that time. It could easily beat a Bf 109E, especially when flown by a skilled pilot. The type was intended to replace the Morane MS-406 however only a few units had been re-equipped with the type by June 1940. Its manoeuvrability and armament, one 20 mm cannon and four machine-guns, made it a dangerous opponent for the Luftwaffe.

The last main fighter came from the USA. France had purchased the export version of Curtiss P-36 to fill the gap between the Morane and the new French designs. The Curtiss was at the end of its development and was close to being declared obsolescent. Its main weakness was its poor armament, only six machine-guns, but nevertheless it performed well against the Luftwaffe (Archives Aero-Editions).

defensive actions against the Luftwaffe. The first true baptism of fire occurred on 26th August when shortly after 1500, Squadron Leader G.D.M. Blackwood took-off with a dozen Hurricanes and at about 1540 they saw fifteen Do17s. The squadron managed to climb 2,000 feet above the bombers and then swept in on the raiders. The first to attack were the Commanding Officer and Sergeant E. Prchal. Both scored a victory but were themselves hit. George Blackwood had to bale out when his wing tanks were hit by return fire, however he was able to land without injury to himself. Prchal´s aircraft was also hit by the escorting Bf109s, and he made an emergency landing five miles north-east of Hornchurch. He was sent to the hospital in Ely as a result of injuries sustained. Those two pilots were the unit's first casualties, but not the last for the day. Pilot Officer Vaclav Bergman was also shot down by Bf109Es and injured but was able to bail out. To balance the books another victory, against a Bf110, was claimed by Pilot Officer Emil Fechtner.

No.310 Squadron continued to fly defensive patrols over the next few days, and on the last day of August Luftwaffe bombers attacked airfields and other RAF facilities. Luftflotte 2 struck at the airfields at Biggin Hill, Croydon, Hornchurch, Debden and Duxford. The latter airfield was hit during the morning but the attackers were chased away by No.19 Squadron. Twelve Hurricanes took off at 1300 and the ground controller directed the squadron, led this time by Flight Lieutenant G. Sinclair, to proceed to Hornchurch at 11,500 feet. Twenty minutes later the pilots of No.310 Squadron met fifteen Do17s escorted by Bf109s. Flight Lieutenant J. Jefferies claimed the first success of the day when he destroyed a Do17Z. This was confirmed by Pilot Officer Stanislav Zimprich who saw the plane going down with its engine on fire. This was subsequently credited as a Do215. At the same time two other Dorniers were destroyed, one fell to Flight Lieutenant G. Sinclair and the other was shot down by Pilot Officer E. Fechtner. The fighter escort then appeared and the game changed. Nevertheless, Flight Lieutenant Jaroslav Maly got one Bf109 but his Hurricane was damaged during the dogfight. Pilot Officer Stanislav Zimprich came out without damage but gained only probable victory over a Bf109. The most successful pilot this day was Squadron Leader Hess who shot down a Bf109 and then a Do17Z (credited as a Do215). The German aircraft crashed on the right bank of the Thames near Eastwick Farm at Burnham-on-Crouch. Two Czechoslovaks also became casualties, Pilot Officer

Three founder members of No.310 Squadron posing in front of Hurricane Mk.I NN-D in September 1940. The Czechoslovak national insignia appeared on both sides of the fuselage. From left to right: Pilot officer O. Posluzny, Sergeants J. Kopriva and K. Kosina. All are wearing RAF uniforms, however Josef Kopriva has kept his French Air Force jacket which he received when he was flying with the French.
(V. Kolesa via P. Vancata)

managed to land their damaged planes. On 12th August Air Vice Marshal Trafford Leigh-Mallory, Officer Commanding No.12 Group, visited the squadron to assess the level of its training. On 17th August the squadron was declared fit for operational duty as a component of No.12 Group and, led by Flight Lieutenant J. Jefferies, the first patrol was carried out. The same day twenty pilots, including Squadron Leader J. Ambrus, were posted to No.6 OTU for re-training however only Pilot Officer Stanislav Fejfar returned to No.310 Squadron. By mid-August the Battle of Britain was raging and on the 20th August 1940, the squadron took-off against the enemy the first time. A section led by Flight Lieutenant Jefferies with his wingmen, Pilot Officers Miloslav Kredba and Vilem Göth, was in the air by 1815. Fifteen minutes later they spotted a lone Do17. They immediately attacked but the enemy escaped into the clouds. The squadron was now participating on a daily basis in

Taken for the propaganda, this official photo of pilots are reading congratulative telegrams at Duxford, September 1940. From left to right : standing Sgt J. Kominek, S/L G. D. M. Blackwood, F/L G. L. Sinclair, F/L J. Maly, Sgt J. Kaucky. upper row: Sgt B. Fürst, Sgt J. Zima, Sgt R. Puda (IWM CH1286)

Miloslav Kredba was shot down by a Bf109 but was able to use his parachute, however Pilot Officer J. Sterbacek was last seen attacking Dorniers over the Thames Estuary. His body was never recovered. Jaroslav Sterbacek thus became the first No.310 Squadron pilot to be killed and the first Czechoslovak in the RAF to die in action.

HOT AUTUMN

The intensity of the Luftwaffe´s raids continued to grow and, on the morning of 3rd September, just after nine o´clock the squadron sent a patrol of four Hurricanes against enemy bombers heading towards North Weald. A quarter of an hour later eight Spitfire Mk.Is of No.19 Squadron took off followed, at 0928, by another six Hurricanes of No. 310 Squadron led by Flight Lieutenant Jefferies. This formation climbed for altitude and at 1035 they saw beneath them, at 21,000 ft, Dorniers of KG 2 escorted by Bf 110s of ZG 2 and ZG 26. As the pilots of the Czechoslovak squadron dived on the enemy the escort turned into the British fighters and the melee became furious. The squadron claimed six confirmed victories and two more probables. Five Bf110s were credited to Flight Lieutenant Jefferies, Pilot Officer Fechtner, Sergeant Josef Koukal, Flight Lieutenant Sinclair and Sergeant Bohumil Fürst. In addition Flight Lieutenant Sinclair shot down a bomber. On the debit side No.310 Squadron lost one Hurricane to Bf110s, flown by Sergeant Josef Kopriva, however he managed to bail out but was slightly injured in the process. Josef Kominek, Jerrard Jefferies and Josef Koukal had to land on North Weald airfield due to a shortage of fuel, however all the other pilots returned safely to base.

Two days later the action went against No.310 Squadron. At 1445 ten Hurricanes led by Flight Lieutenant Jefferies took-off to patrol over North Weald. Green Section, consisting of Pilot Officer Miloslav Kredba, Sergeants Josef Hubacek and Josef Kaucky, bringing up the rear of the formation was attacked by a group of Bf109s. Miroslav Kredba was wounded and had to make a forced landing in his damaged Hurricane which resulted in him having to go to hospital. Josef Kaucky was also shot at, by four Bf109s, but managed to land on Duxford airfield despite his aircraft taking many hits. A bullet tore through one of his boots.

Hawker Hurricane Mk.I P3143, No.310 (Czechoslovak) Squadron, Sergeant B. Fürst, Duxford, 7ᵗʰ September 1940. The Czechoslovakian national insignia were painted on both sides of the cowling. The practice were discontinued by 1941.

On 7th September the Luftwaffe changed its tactics and began attacking British cities and London soon became the main target of the raids. The OC of No.12 Group, Air Vice Marshal Leigh-Mallory began to change the tactics as well. Under the influence of Squadron Leader D. Bader, CO of No.242 (Canadian) Squadron, larger formations were formed by grouping three squadrons into a Wing. The three fighter units based at Duxford were formed into one wing commanded by Douglas Bader. That day, in the afternoon, 348 bombers, escorted by 617 fighters (Bf109s and Bf110s), were launched against London. At 1617 No.11 Group was again called upon to defend London. Bader´s wing took-off at 1700, but his pilots arrived too late to prevent London being bombed and the city was burning. Bader's squadrons caught the retreating invaders. No.242 (Canadian) Squadron attacked first, followed by No.310 Squadron. A dozen Czechoslovaks led by Flight Lieutenant G. Sinclair joined the skirmish with the escorting Bf110s. The leading section was followed by Green Section, led by

Pilot Officer E. Fechtner then Blue and Yellow Sections. The squadron's highest scoring pilot that day was Pilot Officer Vilem Göth who shot down two Bf110s. Sergeant Bohumil Fürst also gained one confirmed and one probable victory. The first one crashed into the sea five miles off Birchington, while the pilot of the second enemy aircraft, a Bf109E, took to his parachute and became a prisoner of war. The squadron claimed six confirmed, three probable victories and four planes damaged for this day. Two of the squadron's planes were lost, Göth´s Hurricane was hit in the glycol tank, obliging him to make a belly landing in a field at Whitman's Farm near Purleigh and while Sergeant Josef Koukal escaped from his burning aircraft serious burns on his face and hands resulted in him spending some time in hospital.

The following day, Pilot Officer Stanislav Fejfar returned to the Squadron having completing his training at No.6 OTU and in the afternoon of the 9th September he made his operational debut. The enemy, 75 Do17s with the escort estimated to 150 Bf110s and

Same group (see page 4) of Czechoslovaks pilots surrounding the three British pilots of No.310 Squadron (F/L G. Sinclair, P/O J.E. Bouton and F/L Jefferies) in September 1940.
From left to right, back row :
P/O V. Bergman, Sgt B. Fürst, Sgt R. Zima, P/O E. Fechtner, P/O S. Zimprich, Sgt J. Kaucky, Sgt K. Seda, F/L J. Maly, P/O V. Göth.
On the front row, on G. Sinclair's right side, Sgt J. Vopalecky, P/O S. Janouch and Sgt R. Puda. (www.ww2images.com)

Bf109s were seen at 1735 over the southern suburbs of London. No.310 Squadron was led into action by Squadron Leader Blackwood however things turned out badly and during a formation change the Hurricanes of Flight Lieutenant Sinclair, and the recently promoted Flying Officer Boulton, collided. Sinclair bailed out but Boulton died in the wreckage of his Hurricane. However just before the crash, his uncontrolled Hurricane knocked down a Bf 110C. In the dogfight which followed No.310 Squadron pilots claimed four confirmed, three probable victories and one plane damaged. All up the Duxford wing claimed 21 victories. Impressed by the results Leigh-Mallory decided to reinforce the wing with No.611 Squadron (Spitfires) and No.302 (Polish) Squadron (Hurricanes).

This new wing went into combat on the 15th September which is now celebrated as Battle of Britain Day. During the morning hundreds of bombers, heavily escorted by fighters, were sighted and all the aircraft in Nos.11 and 12 Groups took off to participate in one of the great air battles of the war.

Led by Douglas Bader, the Duxford Wing took off at 1130. No.310 Squadron, led by Flight Lieutenant Jefferies, climbed towards the German bombers which were soon identified as Dorniers. In little more than a hours fighting, the squadron landed and claimed four victories without loss. An hour and half later they again rose to meet a Luftwaffe force which radar had estimated to be 150 bombers with a strong escort of Bf109s. Contact was made at 1440. Two No.310 Squadron pilots, Squadron Leader A. Hess and Sergeant Josef Hubacek were shot down. Both bailed out safely but Hubacek suffered slight wounds. Despite these losses No.310 Squadron was credited with 4 and 1/2 victories. Fighter Command claimed 185 victories that day even if the score subsequently proved to be more modest.

The 18th September was an other very busy day for the squadron and the wing. After two unfruitful sorties No.310 Squadron took off at 1615 and made contact with the enemy. The Wing was patrolling over Hornchurch, north of London, at an altitude of 23,000 feet when they spotted two groups of enemy bombers heading towards London. Flight Lieutenant Jefferies led the attack with the aim of breaking the enemy formation. During this first attack he shot down one bomber. Five other pilots claimed victories, Pilot Officers Janouch, Fejfar and Vaclav Bergman and Sergeants Jiroudek and Puda however they had all

Group of pilots in front of Hurricane I wearing symbol of squadron CO, Duxford, December 1940.
From left to right : P/O E. Foit (holding dog Mita - squadron mascot), P/O M. Kredba, P/O F. Burda, P/O J. Hybler.
(V. Kolesa via P. Vancata)

Hurricane Mk.I W9323 was taken on charge by No.310 Squadron a short time before the unit receive a batch of Hurricane Mk.II. Only a handful of flights were performed with it in March 1941, flown by the Flight Lieutenant F. Dolezal and Flying Officers J. Hanus and J. Hybler.
(V. Kolesa via P. Vancata)

THE HAWKER **HURRICANE**

The Hawker Hurricane was the first of the RAF's monoplane fighters and the prototype flew for the first time on 6th November 1935.

The initial version, powered by a Merlin II of 1,030 hp, was designated the **Hurricane Mk.I** and was ordered in quantity during the summer of 1936 to rearm the RAF's fighter squadrons. The first aircraft were delivered during the Autumn of 1937 and the type became operational in January 1938. On the eve of the Second World War, nearly 500 Hurricanes had been delivered to the RAF and they were the backbone of Fighter Command until late 1940.

After the Battle of Britain, the Hurricane gave way to the Spitfire as the main fighter of Fighter Command, as squadrons were gradually re-equipped.

It was at that time that the **Hurricane Mk.II**, with the more powerful Merlin XX of 1,390 hp engine appeared, but its performance remained inferior to that of German fighters, and the Hurricane seemed to have reached its limit of development. Because of this the Hurricane I and II would remain the two main production versions.

From mid-1941, the Hurricane was used, briefly, as a night fighter and with more success as a fighter-bomber. Considerable numbers were shipped to other theatres of operations for service in this role however it gradually disappeared from combat in Europe as the RAF introduced new types into service.

However the Hurricane remained in first line service until the end of the war in the Mediterranean, and in the Far East, after which it quickly disappeared from the RAF inventory.

shot at the same aircraft. The squadron's pilots claimed six confirmed and one probable victory that day with only two Hurricanes receiving light damage.

Despite daily patrols the squadron did not meet with the enemy for the nine days until on 27th September at 1155 No.310 Squadron took-off from Duxford and headed towards Canterbury in company with the rest of the Wing. Half an hour later pilots spotted twelve He111s escorted by 30 Bf109s. During the first minutes of the fight Flight Lieutenant Gordon Sinclair was shot down but successfully bailed out. Sergeant Josef Kominek, who at first avoided an attack by Bf109s over Dover, fired on three Bf109s pursuing a Spitfire.

After his third burst the enemy aircraft fell into the sea 5 miles south west of Dover and another success was gained by Pilot Officer Fechtner who then became the most successful Czech pilot of the squadron.

TOWARDS THE END OF THE BATTLE OF BRITAIN

In October the skirmishes with Luftwaffe aircraft became infrequent although the squadron carried out regular patrolling over such bases as Hornchurch, Biggin Hill and Duxford, as well as London. During the month several pilots were posted in to the squadron after the completion of their training at No.6

FIGHTER COMMAND

After experiencing Zeppelin and bomber attacks during the First World War, Britons were well aware that they were vulnerable from the air and the German re-armament programme of the thirties did nothing but further increase this fear. Despite an enlargement process Fighter Command could only boast 25 regular squadrons, two from the special reserve and 12 Auxiliary squadrons when war fell in September 1939. Not only was this number well short of the 57 squadrons deemed necessary for the Air Defence of Great Britain but, of the existing 39, not all were fully operational.

During the first year of the war Fighter Command was expanded somewhat and at the successful conclusion of the Battle of Britain, which would be it's greatest achievement, had almost 70 squadrons on its Battle Order. When the planning for the Invasion of Europe commenced squadrons were divided into defensive and offensive roles and Fighter Command disappeared on 15th November 1943. It was superseded by Air Defence of Great Britain (ADGB), which was responsible for the defence of the British Isles, and the 2nd Tactical Air Force, which pursued the offensive component of the restructure.

At the split-up Fighter Command had approximately 100 squadrons under its umbrella but this was reduced by a third with the inception of the 2nd TAF, which would become the RAF's spearhead for the Invasion. In October 1944 when the advance of Allied troops appeared irreversible, and the Luftwaffe's effort was concentrated mainly on the Eastern front, ADGB re-adopted its original name of Fighter Command. However its needs were not what they had once been and at the German surrender barely 40 squadrons remained under its control.

From its inception Fighter Command was organised into Groups, with geographical boundaries, which would vary in accordance with the changing circumstances of the time. Originally just three Groups, No's 11, 12 and 13 were responsible for the defence of the whole of British Isles, but resources were too thinly spread and by the end of 1940, another three had been re-activated.

Chronologically the Groups were:

No.11 Group: Reformed at Uxbridge on 1st May 1936, it fell under the control of Fighter Command on 14th July. This Group was responsible for the South and, later, the Southeast region of England, which included London. During the Battle of Britain it was situated closest to the enemy and controlled the largest number of squadrons. It went onto the offensive when Fighter Command began attacks across the English Channel in 1941.

No.12 Group: Reformed at Hucknall on 1st April 1937 and was immediately placed under Fighter Command control to defend the central area of England. This included protecting the region located immediately north of No.11 Group, and the Midland industrial area, including the east and west parts south of the Humber.

No.13 Group: Reformed at Newcastle on 15th March 1939 and immediately placed under the control of Fighter Command to ease the pressure on No.12 Group. Its zone initially comprised industrial areas north of the Humber and southern Scotland.

No.10 Group: Reformed at Rudlow Manor on 1st June 1940 primarily to cover the Southwest of England and protect shipping in the western half of the channel. It was absorbed into No.11 Group on 2nd May 1945.

No.14 Group: Reformed at Inverness on 29th June 1940 to protect Scotland. It was absorbed into No.13 Group on 15th July 1943.

No.9 Group: Reformed at Preston on 9th August 1940 to protect the north-west of England and Northern Ireland. It was absorbed into No.12 Group on 15th September 1944.

Sergeant F. Mlejnecky was caught by Bf 109s during a patrol on 5.11.40. He was hit but managed to bring his damaged aircraft back to his base but it overturned while landing. His Hurricane, V7597/NN-D, was repaired and returned to service. (J. Rajlich)

OTU. On 15th October Pilot Officers Hybler, Hanus, Burda, and Sergeants Chalupa, Dvorak and Vindis arrived. The next day three Hurricanes led by Pilot Officer Zaoral, and accompanied by Pilot Officer Hybler and Sergeant Chalupa, took off on a training flight. About thirty minutes later the Hurricane piloted by Chalupa had engine failure and he decided to bail, out however his parachute failed to open and he was killed. By the end of the month other pilots had arrived to reinforce the unit, including Pilot Officer Emil Foit, Sergeants Mlejnecky and Brezovsky, who were posted in on 18th October to replace Pilot Officers Göth, Zaoral, Sergeants Puda and Fürst. The officers went to No.501 Squadron and the NCO's went to No.605 Squadron.

No.310 Squadron's last success during the Battle of Britain occurred on 28th October. Squadron Leader G.D.M. Blackwood led the section, with Flight Lieutenant Maly and Pilot Officer Bergman as his wingmen, to intercept a Do17 spotted shortly before 0800. They located it, fired several bursts and scored hits nevertheless the Dornier escaped into clouds and could only be claimed as damaged. The same day, Squadron Leader Alexander Hess and Pilot Officer Emil Fechtner were awarded the DFC, the first Czechoslovaks in the unit to receive this award. Flight Lieutenant Jefferies had been awarded this medal previously. Alexander Hess and Jefferies were personally decorated by His Majesty King George VI during his visit in Duxford on 15th January 1941 but unfortunately Emil Fechtner was killed the next day in a mid-air collision with Flight Lieutenant Maly's Hurricane.

November started badly. On the 1st, Sergeant Frantisek Vindis lost his way and had to make an emergency landing near Sudbury. He was injured and the plane had to be written off. The next day, during a patrol over the Thames estuary, the Hurricane piloted by Sergeant Kominek caught fire and the pilot had to bail out, but worse was to come on 5th November. No.310 Squadron took off, together with Nos.242 (Canadian) and 19 Squadrons, to patrol between Dover and Canterbury. The Czechoslovaks were jumped by a group of Bf109Es of I./JG 26 and III./JG 26 coming out of the sun and the first Hurricane to be hit was that flown by Sergeant Frantisek Mlejnecky. He managed to return to Duxford where he crashed on landing. Next was Sergeant Puda who had to bail out of his burning plane. Flight Lieutenant Jefferies was forced to make a belly landing at Hornchurch and Sergeant Dvorak crashed at Fowlmere after his engine was damaged. The fifth and last Hurricane to be lost this day was shot down by mistake by British anti-aircraft artillery and Sergeant Miroslav Jiroudek was forced to make a belly landing near Faversham. Five planes lost against no victories, a sad day indeed.

On 14th December President Edvard Benes visited No.310 Squadron and awarded the *Ceskoslovensky valecny kriz* 1939 (Czech War Cross 1939) to some pilots including Squadron Leader G.D.M. Blackwood, the two British flight commanders Flight Lieutenant Jefferies and Sinclair, the Air Base commander Wing Commander Woodhall and posthumously Flying Officer John Boulton.

President Eduard Benes is decorating Sergeant J. Kopriva of the Czechoslovak War Cross on 12th December 1940. Just on his right is standing Sergeant B. Fürst. (via P. Vancata)

NEW YEAR OF FIGHT, NEW COMMANDERS

Early in 1941, G.D.M. Blackwood and Flight Lieutenant Sinclair were posted out and replaced by the newly promoted Squadron Leader Jefferies and a new officer, Flight Lieutenant Patrick B.G. Davies, was posted in. Another officer, the New Zealander M.W.B. Knight was posted in during February to lead the B Flight but he stayed for only a short time. In March, No.310 Squadron changed its Hurricane Mk.Is for the more powerful and better armed Mk.II Nevertheless the activity remained at a low level during the year.

In spring new combat tactics were introduced for Fighter Command. Although the Luftwaffe continued intermittent attacks on Great Britain by night, Fighter Command was switched to carrying out offensive missions over Continental Europe. Nevertheless, as in the first part of 1941 Great Britain still had to be defended by night and training in night fighting continued in Fighter Command units.

Needless to say this activity remained irregular and normal operational patrols were flown regularly. On 25th February, just as Pilot Officer Kredba and Sergeant Hubacek were returning to base from night flying, Duxford airfield was attacked by a lone Ju88. The bomber destroyed a fuel tank and killed two mechanics, AC2 Pohner and LAC Zavadil. Late in

March No.310 Squadron relocated to Coltishall and on the days following the squadron carried out convoy patrols and had occasional contacts with German bombers. One such contact was on the morning of 27th March and a second, night fighting, contact on 8/9 April over Coventry. But no victories were claimed. On 15th May No.310 Squadron' claimed its last victory while flying from Duxford airfield. At noon a convoy patrol, led by the CO Squadron Leader Jerrard Jefferies-Latimer (after his marriage he changed his name from Jefferies to Latimer) and the leader of B flight the Rhodesian Flight Lieutenant Patrick Davies took off. An hour later they spotted a Do17 (actually a Bf110) and shot it down right away. Although most activity was of the routine kind accidents still occurred during this period and on 8th June Sergeant Josef Kominek was killed during a training flight. On 26th June 1941 the squadron left Duxford for Martlesham Heath and came under the command of No.11 Group however its duties remained the same. Squadron Leader Latimer DFC left the squadron on the 8th of June and went to Tangmere where he took command of No.1455 Flight (night fighters) which was later re-numbered No.534 Squadron. He was later killed in action in a Lancaster which failed to return from a raid on Kiel on 5th April 1943. Indeed, during the summer of 1941 the British officers were posted

Hurricane Mk.I V7659 seen at the dispersal in February 1941 at Duxford. Among the pilots who flew this aircraft during the month, there are the New Zealander Flight Lieutenant M.B.W. Knight, Flight Lieutenant F. Dolezal and Flying Officers S. Janouch and J. Hanus. (J. Rajlich)

out and Czechoslovak officers were now fully responsible for the squadron. During the first half of 1941 numerous postings were made and a number of skilled pilots - Fürst, Hubacek, Kaucky, Prchal, Puda, Rechka and Seda left to be replaced by new and younger pilots - Janata, Petr, Popelka, Skach, Srom and Trejtnar.

The stay at Martlesham Heath was short, they remained there for just a month, when they received orders to move to the north of Scotland however during the ferry flight, on 30th July, the Harrow (K6953) from No.271 Squadron which was transporting the men had to make a forced landing in the sea near Montrose following an engine failure. Flight Sergeant Herbert W. Evans, chief of the Squadron's Signal section, drowned before rescuers could arrive. The squadron's new base was Dyce, located north-west of Aberdeen. The missions remained the same, convoy patrols and the defence of Aberdeen against the few Ju88s which

appeared over town. By the end of 1941, the squadron began to convert to Spitfires. The first Spitfires, some old Mk.IIAs arrived at Dyce on 21st October and for a while the squadron had a mixed fleet of Hurricane Mk.IIs, Spitfire Mk.IIs and Mk.Vs. By end of November they had respectively 5, 7 and 13 of each type on charge. During this period only one victory was claimed, by Flying Officer Vaclav Bergman, who during a training flight pursued a lone Ju88. The enemy plane escaped into clouds and it was credited as a probable. Many losses occurred during training or ferry flights and in all the unit lost five planes but fortunately only one pilot. Pilot Officer W. Sniechowski, the sole Pole attached to the squadron, was killed on 8th December 1941 while flying a Spitfire Mk.VB. He had been posted in from No.32 Squadron on 1st June and had participated in the Battle of Britain.

In the middle of December the squadron received orders to relocate to Perranporth but bad weather cau-

---

SERIALS OF HURRICANE II IN USE ON 1ST APRIL 1941.

Z : 2312, 2400, 2488, 2493, 2506, 2524, 2563, 2641, 2643, 2661, 2671, 2693 2766, 2768, 2770, 3909*

Total : 16

*Mk.IIB, otherwise all Mk.IIAs

Ground crew posing in front of Hawker Hurricane Mk.I W9323 in March 1941. By that time No.310 Squadron was waiting for the improved Mk.II version of the Hurricane. Some of the squadron's pilots would have preferred to be flying Spitfires however they had to wait until the end of the year fly one of these aircraft. (J. Rajlich)

sed delays and the transfer was not completed until the 25th. No.310 Squadron switched with No.66 Squadron and became part of No.10 Group. Operational flying began on 27th December.

ROUTINE AND ROUTINE AGAIN !

The main task of the squadron was once again convoy patrols, alert standbys against Luftwaffe reconnaissance planes, and covering the return of No.1 PRU's Spitfires from reconnaisance sorties. Returning from a combat patrol over a convoy on 11th January 1942 Squadron Leader Frantisek Weber, the CO, and Flying Officer Bohumil Kimlicka collided while landing. Both pilots survived but unfortunately for Weber his injuries brought about the end of his career as an operational fighter pilot. On 4th February a section led by Flight Lieutenant Frantisek Burda took-off to intercept a Ju88. After half an hour Sergeant Zdenek Skarvada reported that his engine was running irregularly and he became separated from the rest of the patrol. On their return to base the B flight commander, Flight Lieutenant Kredba, ordered to four pilots to search for the missing pilot. They did not find the pilot however they met a lone Ju88 and inflicted damaged on it. Two weeks later, on 22nd February, a message was received advising them that Skarvada had become a prisoner of war, the first for the No.310 Squadron. He could bail out in the vicinity of Scilly Island and was rescued by a German ship.

This was not the only loss this month as, on 14th February, Flight Lieutenant Miloslav Kredba was killed during a training flight. In March 1942, the Squadron flew a limited number of sorties, both operational and training. On 12th April 1942 six B flight pilots were on a training flight when Flight Lieutenant Zimprich flew too close to Sergeant Stanislav Halama and damaged the fin of Halama's aircraft. Halama rapidly lost the height and tried to make a forced landing which unfortunately was unsuccessful and he was killed in the crash. Zimprich tried to land on the beach but landed 350 yards off shore and disappeared. Prompt rescue action was unsuccessful and Zimprich´s body was not found until 14th July 1942. On 7th April Squadron Leader Frantisek Dolezal became the CO of No.310 Squadron which he had unofficially led since 11th January when Squadron Leader Weber was injured.

Under Dolezal´s command No.310 Squadron, now part of Portreath Wing, escorted Hurricanes and Whirlwinds on raids against targets in France and German ships in the Channel. After a long wait the unit claimed a confirmed victory on the evening of 28th April when Blue Section shot down a reconnaissance Ju88 over a convoy. The claim was shared between Flight Lieutenant E. Foit and Flight Sergeant F. Vindis. Early in May the Czechoslovak fighter wing was formed and based at Exeter. Its first CO was Wing Commander Alois Vasatko, former CO of No.312 Squadron and a French Air Force veteran. The

Hawker Hurricane Mk.IIA Z2770, No.310 (Czechoslovak) Squadron, Flight Lieutenant B. Kimlicka, Duxford, March 1941.
The pre-war Czechoslovakian Air Force insignia was painted on the nose of this machine which was unusual for two reasons. This was more commonly painted near the cockpit and secondly it was rarely painted on any of No.310 Squadron's aircraft. Another unusual feature was the individual aircraft letter painted under the nose which was also rarely used in this unit.

Flying Officer F. Burda at readiness seated in the Hurricane IIA Z2768/NN-H during Summer 1941 at Duxford. This machine was one of the first to be taken on charge by No.310 Squadron in March 1941. (V. Kolesa via P. Vancata)

squadron moved to Exeter on 7ᵗʰ May. The Wing was placed under No.10 Group's authority and was comprised Nos.310, 312 and 154 Squadrons. The first Czechoslovak Wing operation - *Rodeo* 11 - was scheduled to take place on 29ᵗʰ May but bad weather cancelled the mission. This took place on the 1ˢᵗ of June when, together with Ibsley Wing, led by Wing Commander I.R. "Widge" Gleed, the Exeter (Czechoslovak) Wing, went into action.

The squadron claimed its first success as part of the new Wing on 5ᵗʰ June during *Circus* 7. Together with No.154 Squadron, the unit took off from Bold Head to escort Bostons to the airfield at La Morlaix. At 1510 they were attacked by eight FW190s, and in the following melee the squadron damaged five enemy aircraft and returned home without any losses at 1540, but one Spitfire, Sergeant Jaroslav Chlup's aircraft, was damaged.

Five days later the squadron was again successful

against Fw190s. The Czechoslovak Wing, which with the arrival of No.313 Squadron now consisted of three Czechoslovak fighter units, took-off to take part in *Circus* 9. They had to escort Bostons of No.107 Squadron to raid Lannion airfield, in France. On the return flight Czechoslovak pilots engaged a number of German aircraft, and claimed three planes destroyed, one probable and one damaged without losses. The German broke through to the British bombers and one was lost to a FW190.

A couple of days later, in the evening of 16ᵗʰ June, a section of No.310 Squadron attacked a reconnaissance Ju88D which approached a convoy near Bridgeport and damaged it. The pilot of this Junkers made a crash landing on Lannion airfield and the crew survived.

On 23ʳᵈ June, the Czechoslovak Wing took part in the *Ramrod* 23. This action brought a good return for the RAF. At 1815, 36 Spitfires, twelve from each squadron, took off from Exeter airfield. No.310 Squadron

SERIALS OF SPITFIRE V IN USE ON 1ˢᵀ JANUARY 1942.

AD : 328, 331, 365, 366, 374, 378, 382, 412, 414, 420, 422, 423, 453, 462, 464, 582

Total : 16

CODENAMES - OFFENSIVE OPERATIONS

CIRCUS :
Bombers heavily escorted by fighters, the purpose being to bring enemy fighters into combat.

RAMROD :
Bombers escorted by fighters, the primary aim being to destroy a target.

RANGER :
Large formation freelance intrusion over enemy territory with aim of wearing down enemy figthers.

RHUBARD :
Freelance fighter sortie against targets of opportunity.

RODEO :
A fighter sweep without bombers.

SWEEP :
An offensive flight by fighters designed to draw up and clear the enemy from the sky.

was led by Squadron Leader Frantisek Dolezal and the Wing escorted six Bostons on another raid on Morlaix airfield. The target was protected by heavy *flak* and just after the bombs were dropped the formation was attacked by FW190s. After a furious combat between the fighters one of the Bostons was shot down. At the beginning of the fight Flight Lieutenant Foit shot down one FW190, however the Germans tried to prevent their withdrawal and at 1935 they were attacked six miles south of Start Point. Ten FW190s picked on No.312 Squadron led by Wing Commander Vasatko and as he turned sharply to the right he collided with a Focke-Wulf. The German pilot bailed out but Vasatko was killed. The fight continued back over the Channel to the British coast. With the aim of helping the returning formation, four

Sergeant J. Chlup standing in front of Spitfire VB BL710/NN-V during the spring of 1942. This machine made its first sortie, a patrol, on 6th March 1942 with F. Burda at the controls. Except for the leaders of the squadron, the Czechoslovaks do not seem to have been issued with their "own" aircraft and flew whatever aircraft was available. (J. Rajlich)

A group of Spitfires VBs at Perranporth airfield in the spring of 1942 taxiing out for another mission. No personal insignia can be seen on those aircraft which would identify the pilots as Czechoslovakian. (V. Kolesa via P. Vancata).

Spitfires from Nos.310 and 312 Squadrons tried to take off. Unfortunately, a collision occurred on the runway and only Flight Sergeants Tomas Motycka (No.312 Squadron) and Frantisek Trejtnar (No.310 Squadron) became airborne. Later, as both pilots returned to the base, and just after Motycka had landed, Trejtnar saw a lone FW190 flying about 1,000 feet above him. In spite of his disadvantageous position he decided to climb and engage the enemy. Trejtnar climbed into the sun and decoyed the enemy inland. Nevertheless, the German had still superiority of altitude and shot him down, however he was able to bail out but on landing he broke a leg. All was not lost as the victor, *Oberleutnant* Armin Faber the *Gruppenadjutant* of III./JG 2, landed by mistake on Pembrey airfield and the RAF gained an undamaged specimen of FW190A.

Bad weather for most of July nearly stopped offensive sorties over the Continent and the squadron switched to boring convoy patrols. On 23rd July 1942, No.310 Squadron participated in *Rhubarb* 85, in conjunction with No.313 Squadron, and again attacked Lannion and La Morlaix airfields. No.310 Squadron's target was Lannion and they destroyed one Ju88 on the ground and damaged another. German *Flak* damaged three Spitfires in the process

but their pilots, Sergeants Josef Stivar, Antonin Skach and Flight Sergeant Leopold Srom returned to base safely. A week later the whole Czechoslovak Wing twice escorted Hurribombers to attack ships near Les Sept Isles and Batz Island. Next day, on 31st July, shortly after taking off for an operation over Saint Malo, Flight Lieutenant Bohuslav Kimlicka had an engine failure and he tried to land on top of a cliff but his plane didn't make it and was destroyed. Kimlicka was unhurt.

OPERATION *JUBILEE*

For Operation *Jubilee*, the raid on Dieppe on 19th August 1942, the RAF supplied tactical support and air cover for the landings which took place around the town. To prepare for the mission No.310 Squadron moved from Exeter to Redhill airfield. This base was the home of Nos.350 (Belgian) and 611 Squadrons and during Operation *Jubilee* became the host of two other units No.303 (Polish) Squadron and No.312 (Czechoslovak) Squadron, both flying Spitfires. Readiness on Redhill was ordered for 0347 on the 19th, and the Czechoslovak squadrons took-off for the first mission at 0755 with Wing Commander Karel Mrazek DFC leading 24 Spitfires. Ten minutes later they joined up with 24 Hurricanes of Nos.3 and 43 Squadrons led by Squadron Leaders Berry and Le Roy du Vivier, a Belgian. Their targets were E-boats which operated from Boulogne. Except for a number of fishing boats and a 500 ton merchant ship no vessels were seen, so they flew direct to Dieppe. All the aircraft came back safely with the last Spitfire landing at 0935. After re-arming and refuelling No.310 Squadron took off for its second sortie at 1023 followed by No.350 (Belgian) Squadron. When they arrived over Dieppe they joined up with 307th Fighter Squadron, USAAF. All the squadrons attacked German bombers escorted by FW190s and the Spitfires showed no mercy to the bombers and No.310 Squadron claimed three Do217s as probably destroyed. Another ten planes, eight Do217s and two FW190s were claimed as damaged by Czechoslovak pilots. The squadron returned to Redhill airfield at 1155, quite satisfied with this mission. Shortly after 1400 the Squadron took off for the third time to give cover to returning ships. No incidents were reported. The CO, Squadron Leader Frantisek "Dolly" Dolezal was was awarded the DFC for his efforts and actions in the course of Operation *Jubilee*. The rest of the month remained quiet, only one kill being claimed on 28th

BREAKDOWN OF THE PERSONNEL ON 30TH APRIL 1942		
CATEGORY	CZECH	BRITISH
Officers Pilots	6	-
Officers Ground	7	3
Warrant Officer	2	-
W/O ground	1	1
NCO pilots	18	-
NCO ground	32	6
Other ranks	111	35

August when Squadron Leader Dolezal shared a confirmed victory with Wing Commander Karel Mrazek. Both took-off against bandits over Bridgeport and contact was made five minutes later over Exmouth. After accuracy bursts from both pilots the reconnaissance Bf109 of 1(F)./123 crashed into the sea 6 miles south of Exmouth. By this time, combating surprise attacks by fighter-bombers from the Jabo units had became the main task of squadrons based in the south of England.

In September the squadron lost two pilots. On 11th Sergeant Karel Janata disappeared shortly after take off for a weather-recconnaissance flight over the French coast and on 22nd it was the turn of Sergeant

Redhill during Operation *Jubilee,* some pilots of No.310 Squadron in readiness
First from left F/Sgt Karel Pernica (who scored over Dieppe), fifth from left (semi-profile with Mae West) F/Sgt Frantisek Vindis (later DFC recipient). Centre (with officer's cap and Mae West) F/Lt Vladislav "Chocho" Chocholin who also scored over Dieppe, and third from right S/L Frantisek "Dolly" Dolezal also scored over Dieppe. He will later lead the wing and awarded the DSO and DFC. The fourth from right S/L Dr. Zdenek "Doc" Vitek, the squadron's medical officer, and on his left, S/O Dolores "Dolly" Sperkova, war correspondent. She later became Dolores Prchalova when she married with ex-310 Sqn ace Eduard Prchal. The seventh from right (from profile with Mae West) is W/O Adolf Fornusek who also scored over Dieppe. (J. Rajlich)

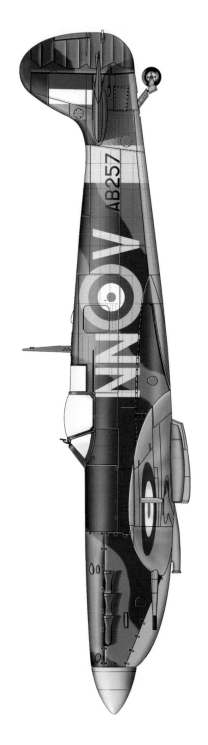

Supermarine Spitfire Mk.VB AB257, No.310 (Czechoslovak) Squadron, Flight Lieutenant E. Foit, Perranporth, February 1942.

Arnost Stanek who, during *Rhubarb* 89, was hit by flak and crahed killing the pilot. A couple of weeks later Pilot Officer Jan Doucha met the same fate on 7th November 1942. That day No.310 Squadron escorted B-17s of 306th Bomb Group on a raid on the submarine base at Brest. Suddenly two FW190s attacked and hit Doucha´s aircraft. The counter-attacks by Flight Lieutenants Foit and Chocholin were unsuccessful and, with his engine trailing smoke, Doucha turned back to England. Unfortunately he failed to reach land and had to bail out 20 miles south of Predannack. The rescue action was unsuccessful and his body was found on 21st December on a shore in South Wales. These were the last unit losses in 1942.

YEAR OF TRANSITION

Even though Winter allowed only a few days for operational flying the squadron was kept very busy during January 1943, not only with the ongoing offensive over the Continent, but also scrambles against low flying attacking fighter-bombers which had became the Germans main offensive tactic against Britain in 1943. On 2nd January two pilots, Pilot Officers Karel Zouhar and Ladislav Zadrobilek, took-off to intercept six FW190s which had attacked Torquay. They engaged them in combat without result and Zadrobilek came back with an injured left hand. A couple of days later, in the middle of January, changes occurred at the head of the squadron with Emil Foit becoming the new CO. On 29th January another combat took place during *Ramrod* 50. That day the Czechoslovak Wing escorted twelve Bostons to bomb the viaduct at Morlaix. The attack was successful and the formation was returning to England when, suddenly, the rear section of Bostons was attacked by nine FW190s. A furious combat arose between the Germans and the Czechoslovaks. At the end of the day the Czechoslovaks claimed two FW190s destroyed, one probably destroyed and two damaged. But it was not one sided as this success cost the lives of Warrant Officers Sala and Petr and the Czechoslovaks could not prevent the loss of one Boston to the FW190s.

February was quiet but it ended quite badly for No.310 Squadron and the Czechoslovak Wing. On 27th February 1943, Nos.310 and 313 Squadrons shifted to the airfield at Predannack and it was from this airfield that 21 Spitfire Mk.Vs provided the forward escort of 63 American B-17s and 15 B-24s. This raid

In 1942 the Spitfire Mk.V became the most commonly used British fighter. No.310 Squadron fought with this version for two years. Spitfire AR503 was taken on charge early in August 1942 and was first flown by Sergeant L. Valousek. During Operation Jubilee it was flown by Flight Lieutenant V. Chocholin. (J. Rajlich)

was against the U-boat base in the harbour of Brest. The mission began badly as five Spitfires had to return early to base because of mechanical problems leaving only 16 Spitfires to continue the escort mission. Over the target the bombers arrived 30 minutes late and the top cover, the Portreath Wing, failed to arrive and the squadron became the target for anti-aircraft fire. Flight Lieutenant Burda's Spitfire was hit in the right wing and he had no choice but to bail out and become a prisoner of war. The two Czechoslovak fighter units attacked the FW190s however the Germans got two more Spitfires. No.310 Squadron lost Flight Lieutenant Vaclav Ridkosil, Flight Lieutenant F. Stusak of No.313 Squadron was also shot down. Squadron Leader J. Himr, the CO of No.313 Squadron claimed one FW190 as damaged Not a good day for the squadron.

The Spitfire Mk.V could not match the performance of the FW190, and the new Spitfire Mk.IX, which had a much better performance was available in insufficient quantities to re-equip all the front line squadrons. It had became very hard to gain the successes with the Mk.Vs and the losses of men and machines increased. By 26th June 1943, when the entire Czechoslovak Wing left Exeter, No.310 Squadron had lost three pilots, among them were Flying Officer Otto Pavlu and Warrant Officer Karel Körber, both veterans of combats in France, and four planes. In addition three Spitfires were damaged and one pilot

injured. The only success during this period was gained by the squadron on 24th June during *Circus* 38 when two FW190s were claimed as damaged while escorting Mitchells on a raid to Guipavas airfield.

Two days later the Squadron moved north to Castletown airfield in Scotland. Pilots and ground personnel were once again ferried on board Harrows of No.271 Squadron. The aerial defence of Scapa Flow, base of the Home Fleet, was to be the main task of the unit. Soon afterwards, at the end of July, Czech pilots began to receive a new mark of Spitfire, the HF Mk.VIs, most of which were inherited from No.313 Squadron. During their stay in Scotland pilots of No.310 Squadron did encounter any enemy aircraft. On the 19th September, No.504 Squadron arrived to replace No.310 Squadron which left their Spitfire Mk.VIs to the newcomers. Next day the squadron moved to Ibsley, where the Czechoslovak squadrons formed the Ibsley Wing. No.310 Squadron took over the planes of the departing No.131 Squadron.

In preparation for D-Day

In the following weeks the Czechoslovak Wing was busy escorting American B-26 Marauders and A-20 Havocs of 8th and 9th Air Force, and British Mitchells and Bostons of 2nd Tactical Air Force on the raids against the Luftwaffe airfields in Northern France. The next contact with enemy aircraft occurred on 24th

Levelled on trestles for gun harmonisation, Spitfire Mk.IX MH819/NN-M is seen wearing full D-Day markings with the serial painted above the fin flash. The participation of the Czechoslovaks in the first phase of liberation of Europe was short, as the Czechoslovakian Wing being transferred to ADGB before the end of June 1944. (www.ww2images.com)

Spitfire Mk.VB EP464/NN-E was first shared between Sergeant V. Popelka and Flight Sergeant F. Mlejnecky when the machine was taken on charge on 01.08.42. But a couple of days later, during Operation *Jubilee*, it was the mount of Flight Lieutenant B. Kimlicka. (www.ww2images.com)

THE SUPERMARINE SPITFIRE

The Supermarine Spitfire was the main RAF fighter during World War II, and the only British fighter to remain in production throughout. It made its maiden flight on 5th March 1936 powered by a Rolls-Royce 990 hp Merlin C engine. Suitably impressed, the Air Ministry placed an order in July and mass production of the Spitfire Mk.I, powered with a Rolls-Royce Merlin II 1,030 hp engine, commenced.

It entered service in August 1938 and ten squadrons were operational at the outbreak of war. During the Battle of France a few Spitfires flew reconnaissance flights, although its first serious test took place during the evacuation of Dunkirk.

During the Battle of Britain it proved superior to the Hurricane and was to remain the RAF's principal fighter until the end of the war. The improved **Spitfire Mk.II**, powered by a 1,175 hp Merlin XII, appeared in August 1940 and was, in turn, replaced by the **Spitfire Mk.V** during the spring of 1941. This version, powered by a 1,470 hp Merlin 45, was better armed and was the first of the two dominant variants of the Spitfire. It did however have serious problems contending with the FW190 when it subsequently appeared.

The **Spitfire Mk.IX**, the second major variant (1,650 hp Merlin 63) arrived in July 1942, to arrest the situation for the RAF, but it was not until well into 1943 that it appeared in sufficient enough numbers to gain a measure of superiority.

In the meantime, the **Spitfire Mk.VI** had been put into service in limited numbers. Based on the Mk.V airframe, it was specifically intended for high altitude combat and was fitted with a pressurised cockpit, increased span wings and a Merlin 47 of 1,415 hp. It proved to be operationally unsatisfactory.

A second generation of Spitfires appeared during 1944, when the Rolls-Royce Griffon engine, capable of delivering upwards of 2,000 hp, was developed. However these only partially replaced the Merlin-powered marks already in service.

From March 1942 Spitfires were sent overseas in increasing numbers and by the end of the war were present in all RAF theatres of operation. Both generations of Spitfire were widely used in the post-war RAF until jet aircraft fully replaced them during the early fifties.

2ᴺᴰ TACTICAL AIR FORCE

Following the Desert Air Force's success in North Africa, in its support of the British 8th Army, the RAF decided to create a similar structure to support ground forces that were gathering in the British Isle to carry out the planned Invasion of Europe. This resulted in the creation of the 2nd Tactical Air Force on 1st June 1943 with the RAF having to draw upon elements of Fighter, Bomber and Army Co-Operation Commands, to form the new command. Army Co-operation Command was considered obsolete and effectively dissolved.

Plans for the invasion began to gain momentum in the spring of 1943 after the surrender of the Axis forces in North Africa had freed up Allied troops. Until then the RAF in Britain had been organised in such a way that only Army Co-operation Squadrons were able to give direct support to the Army. Initially the 2nd Tactical Air Force was responsible to Fighter Command, but it became fully autonomous on 15th November and fell under the structure of the newly formed Allied Expeditionary Air Force. The task allocated to 2nd TAF was simple- it was to provide support to the 21st Army Group, which incorporated all the Commonwealth ground units that were to take part in the invasion. This Army Group was itself divided into two Armies - the 2nd British and the 1st Canadian.

By D-Day, the 2nd Tactical Air Force consisted of :

<u>No.2 Group</u> : Formerly part of Bomber Command its ten light and medium bomber squadrons, which specialised in daylight bombing, were transferred to 2nd TAF control on 1st June 1943. At the time its squadrons were equipped with Bostons, Mitchells and Venturas, although those operating Venturas were fully re-equipped with Mosquito FB.VIs by September. By the time the invasion began No.2 Group had been enlarged to 12 squadrons arranged under four Wings.

<u>No.83 Group</u> : Created on 1st April 1943 as part of Fighter Command, it passed into 2nd TAF control on 1st June 1943. Its role was to provide support to the 2nd British Army and by D-Day it consisted of 29 combat squadrons, under ten Wings, and four Air Observation Post (AOP) Squadrons, under an 11th Wing.

<u>No.84 Group</u> : Created on the 15th July 1943 to give aerial support to the 1st Canadian Army. By D-Day it consisted of 29 combat squadrons under 10 Wings, and three AOP Squadrons under an 11th Wing.

<u>No85 Group</u> : Created on the 2nd December 1943, to provide aerial protection, particularly at night, to that region in which the Invasion force was being prepared. By D-Day this Group consisted of 12 combat squadrons (an even mix of night and day fighters) arranged under five Wings. It also included an Air Spotting Pool containing a further seven squadrons - four from the Fleet Air Arm, one from the US Navy and two Tactical Reconnaissance - and a Flight. By October 1944 the Battle line had moved well away from UK bases and this Group was relegated a Maintenance and Training Group.

<u>No.87 Group</u> : Created on 17th February 1945 to take over control of units in the Paris and Southern French zones.

<u>Headquarters</u> : Headquarters 2nd TAF also had under its umbrella a three-squadron Reconnaissance Wing and a Meteorological Flight.

SERIALS OF SPITFIRE VI IN USE ON 1ˢᵗ SEPTEMBER 1943.

BR : 189, 252, 297, 304, 577, 579
BS : 141, 146, 437, 442, 465, 472

Total : 12

September 1943 when the Wing, led by Wing Commander Dolezal, was escorting twelve Mitchells to the airfield at Poulmic-Lauvéoc and the seaplane base in Brest Harbour. Blue section of No.310 Squadron, led by Flight Lieutenant Chocholin, found itself in combat with the Bf110s of II./ZG 1. The section leader and Flying Officer Stanislav Masek shot down one Bf110 but return fire hit Flight Lieutenant Chocholin's aircraft which disappeared into the Channel 15 miles north of Ouessant. Three days later, early in the morning, the wing moved to Tangmere and at 1000 took-off to escort 72 B-26 bombers of the 322ⁿᵈ and 387ᵗʰ Bombardment Groups to Beauvais-Tillé airfield. The Luftwaffe took off to intercept the bombers, but the Czechs prevented them closing on the bombers and in the following melee Flight Lieutenant Karel Drbohlav claimed one FW190 as a probable.

Early in November the Czechoslovak Wing was renamed No.134 (Czechoslovak) Airfield and was incorporated into the 2ⁿᵈ Tactical Air Force, then on 7ᵗʰ January into No.84 Group of the 2ⁿᵈ TAF. A week later Squadron Leader Hugo Hrbacek became the squadrons new commanding officer. Another change took place that month when, on 20ᵗʰ January 1944, the first Spitfire IXs were taken on charge by the squadron. The conversion to the new type was completed by 8ᵗʰ February. The two other sister-squadrons were also re-equipped with Spitfire Mk.IXs and No.134 (Czechoslovak) Airfield was re-named No.134 (Czechoslovak) Wing shortly before D-Day. After their conversion to the new aircraft the Wing went to Mendlesham airfield.

In connection with the preparations for D-Day the squadron began dive bomber training which was fitted in between operational flying. On 3ʳᵈ April 1944 all the Czechoslovak squadrons took up residence at Appledram airfield. Many sorties were flown in April however no losses were recorded that month although a few aircraft were hit by *flak*. On 21ˢᵗ April the whole Wing took-off to bomb the V-1 flying bomb launch sites near Abbeville. All planes returned from *Ramrod 764* with only the Spitfire Mk.IX flown by Flight Sergeant Miroslav Moravec being damaged by *flak*. Five days later, after returning from Exercise *Lambourne II*, Pilot Officer Vojtech Lysicky crashed his Spitfire and was killed. The 21ˢᵗ of May was a black day for No.134 (Czechoslovak) Wing. Shortly after 1000, 36 Spitfires took off in four plane sections for *Ramrod* 905. The targets were railway bridges, viaducts and locomotives. The Wing lost no less than four planes and another nine returned with various degrees of damage. Red Section attacked an armoured train near Lisieux. The *flak* was very accurate and hit the Spitfire piloted by Squadron Leader Hrbacek who made a crash landing on a field south of Lissieux and managed to avoid capture. He was put in contact with the Maquis and on 18ᵗʰ August 1944 he crossed the

---

SERIALS OF SPITFIRE IX IN USE ON 15ᵀᴴ MARCH 1944.

MH : 938
MJ : 291, 509, 530, 605, 663, 714, 722, 798, 825, 829, 888, 906
MK : 116, 150, 228, 242, 304

Total : 18

---

front line and returned to Great Britain.

Yellow Section attacked trains in the railway station at Vire and lost Pilot Officer Karel Valasek when he crashed in the woods close to Balleroy. He was later captured on 21st August trying to cross front-line near Villers Bocage. Anti-aircraft fire also hit the Spitfire flown by Sergeant Augustin Meier of Blue Section and the plane and pilot disappeared in the sea north of Grandcamp.

D-DAY AT LAST!

The highlight of the squadron's combat activities in 1944 was its participation on the invasion to France. On D-Day, 6th June 1944, the squadron achieved forty-eight sorties, in four missions, but it did not encounter the enemy until the 8th. The first sortie occurred in the morning of 6th June at 0720 when the Czechoslovak Wing was led personally by the Sector Commander, Group Captain A.G. "Sailor" Malan. The squadron patrolled over Juno Beach however the next day began tragically. Shortly after take off Flight Sergeant Miroslav Moravec had to return to base because of mechanical trouble and, tragically, he crashed in a field south-east of Appledram and was killed. The other missions were accomplished without incident.

As previously mentioned the first skirmish with the enemy occurred on 8th June. At 1220 36 Spitfires took-off to patrol over the Normandy Beachhead. The enemy was seen at 1335 and a furious combat ensued with 12 FW190 fighter bombers of II./JG 4. One FW190 was shot down by Flying Officer Otto Smik, the top scoring Czechoslovak fighter pilot of this period. The next claim made by the squadron occurred in the evening of the 17th when the squadron was led by Flight Lieutenant F. Bernard on a patrol over the Normandy Beachhead. The section led by Otto Smik separated from the formation to identify floating object in the sea which proved to be an external fuel tank. When Smik's section returned to the formation they heard the report of bandits located south of Caen. His section was directed to this zone and he saw two FW190s at about 10,500 feet. Smik attacked from out of the sun and in his first attack he shot down one FW190. The second plane was attacked by Flying Officer Vindis and this was severely damaged. Subsequently Smik attacked the FW190 and destroyed it, sharing the claim with Vindis.

Before being sent to France, No.134 (Czechoslovak) Wing received Spitfire LF Mk.IXEs and on 28th June the Czechoslovaks landed on the airfield B-10 (Plumetôt), a meadow 6 kilometres north of Caen. After four years the Czechoslovaks had finally returned to France. At 1600 that day the squadron took-off on an armed-recconnaissance sortie. That night the airfield became the target of German 88 mm artillery but this caused no major damage. Next day No.310

Spitfire Mk.IX MH843 seen at North Weald in autumn 1944. At that time it was being flown by Squadron Leader Jiri Hartman. Note the Squadron code NN has been painted ahead of the roundel on the right side instead of at the rear of it. (J. Rajlich)

RECRUITMENT PROBLEMS

Even though the Czechoslovaks, like the Poles, had arrived in the United Kingdom during the summer of 1940, in sufficient numbers to form three Squadrons (two fighters and one bomber), the Czechoslovakian Government in exile were soon to be faced with a recruiting problem. Although the number of Air Force personnel remained constant from 1940 to 1944 at around 1,600 men and women there was a critical lack of ground crew. In July 1940 about 575 flying personnel arrived in the United Kingdom but only 250 mechanics. The Czechoslovaks had been numerous enough to fight alongside the French, and at one point they had been able to raise an Infantry division, so it would seem that many of these men chose voluntary demobilisation after the Armistice. The airmen who came to the United Kingdom in the summer of 1940 were either flying officers or senior NCOs instead of the lower ranks. The shortage of the latter was to plague the CzAF throughout the war. As early as 1941, the problem was raised by both the RAF and the CIG as it was obvious that new personnel would be needed to replace losses, or just to allow a turn over of personnel in the operational units. As it was, the Czechoslovakian units were dramatically lacking in ground crew from their own nation and this, at a later date, was to jeopardise the existence of No.313 Squadron despite there being enough Czechoslovakian pilots available to be posted in. In February 1941 85% of the ground crew in No.310 Squadron were Czechoslovaks, but only 50% in the case of No.312 Squadron. In these conditions a political agreement was signed to allow the creation of No.313 Squadron with the majority of its ground crew coming from British sources and this led to the establishment of a full Czechoslovak fighter wing. The RAF insisted that Czechoslovak Army personnel enlist in the RAF as ground crew for No.313 Squadron, however the Czechoslovak Government in exile was against this idea as their Army was also facing problems in obtaining men to maintain its numbers. The Army was too small to be involved in any large scale actions and was limited to just Middle East operations.

As replacement personnel could not be obtained from Czechoslovakia, other sources were tried. Three were investigated, two countries in North America, Britain and the land forces in the Middle East. The Czechoslovakian Government had real hopes of obtaining volunteers from Canada, but the Canadians did not encourage any Czechoslovaks, nor Poles for that matter, to enlist in the RAF. Only a handful of men were recruited in Canada and the United States of America mainly because of lack of publicity and political support from Canada or the United Kingdom. It also proved difficult to motivate people to fight for a country they had chosen to leave many years previously. For those reasons the Czechoslovak units had to be used carefully, to avoid seeing the units disbanded due to a lack of personnel. However their fighting spirit remained intact throughout the war and if their military value was less than could have been obtained the publicity given to the Czechoslovakian units played a major role in the political field.

Squadron took-off twice to strike at ground targets and during the second sortie Sergeant Jiri Bauer was posted missing. The same day, the whole was transferred to ADGB. This decison was taken due to a shortage of Czech pilots and the inability to maintain strengh with projected 2nd TAF casualty rates. The personel of No.310 Squadron, together with other units of the Czechoslovak Wing, returned to Great Britain arriving at their new base at Lympe and, over the next few days, the squadron escorted Lancasters and Halifaxes on raids over France.

The pilots also took part in several anti-diver, V-1, patrols. In the evening of 8th July, Flying Officer Smik and Flying Officer Josef Pipa took off on one such patrol. In the course of this patrol Smik destroyed three doodlebugs, but as Pipa's guns jammed, he could not fire a shot! This failure was rectified and when he again took-off his guns were operational and he destroyed a V-1 over the Channel, east of Folkestone. On 11th July the Czechoslovak Wing was pulled out of the line for a rest period. No.310 relocated to the airfield at Digby in Lincolnshire, where it

replaced No.504 Squadron and took over their Spitfire LF Mk.VBs. Two days later B Flight was sent to Hutton Cranswick airfield in Yorkshire, however little flying was undertaken. This did not satisfy the pilots so that they voluntarily carried out Ranger sorties over the occupied Netherlands. In the course of one such action two pilots, Flying Officer Stanislav Masek and Sergeant Arnost Elbogen shot down a Do217 night fighter near Nijmegen on the evening of 8th August. This was not only the last victory scored by No.310 Squadron but also the last enemy plane destroyed in the air by Czechoslovak pilots serving in the RAF during World War Two. Unfortunately on 11th August, during another *Ranger* sortie, Sergeant Elbogen brushed the wing of his Spitfire against a tree while attacking a train near Zaltbommel, and was killed in the crash.

LAST MISSIONS, LAST LOSSES
On 28th August, the unit arrived at North Weald where it joined No.312 (Czechoslovak) Squadron. Both

Another Spitfire Mk.IX during Winter 1944-1945. Even if the serial is not readable, it could be MH330 which was in use at the end of March 1945. (IWM HU40528)

squadrons were immediately ordered to escort *Ramrod* 1244, a raid by Halifaxes and Lancasters on the V-1 launch sites between Lille and Ghent. No.310 Squadron was still flying Spitfire Mk.VBs but next day it received Spitfire F Mk.IXs. The main task of the squadron, until the end of the war was escorting bombers of the RAF to the Netherlands and in Germany and losses continued to mount up. On 31st August, during *Ramrod* 1251, Flight Sergeant Frantisek Rehor, who had probably lost orientation when he flew into the clouds, crashed into the sea. The same reason probably occasioned the death of Warrant Officer Antonin Skach who crashed near St. Michael on 3rd September during *Ramrod* 1258. Two days later the anti-aircraft fire near Breuketen caused the loss of two men and planes, Flying Officer Rostislav Kanovsky was saved by his parachute but became a prisoner of war and Warrant Officer Antonin Kaminek, who also made an emergency landing, managed to avoid capture. With the help of the Dutch Underground he crossed the front line on 13th December and returned to the unit.

In the middle of September Jiri Hartman succeeded Vaclav Raba as CO. Soon afterwards, on 17th September, Operation *Market Garden*, an airborne operation to capture the Dutch bridges over the Rhine, was launched. No.310 Squadron was part of the escort

for transports and gliders. The first sortie started from North Weald at 1215 and on this occasion the squadron fired at artillery batteries at Standaarbirish. Despite the best efforts of all who took part in Market Garden the operation, which ended on 26th September, was a disaster. In Autumn 1944, escorting Allied bombers to targets in Germany were the most frequent missions asked of the squadron and the Czechoslovak Wing operated from such continental bases as B-65 Maldeghem, B-67 Ursel, B-86 Helmond and B-90 Petit Brogel. On 29th December the Squadron was transferred to Bradwell Bay airfield. During the escort flights clashes with enemy planes were rare and the squadron's losses were caused by anti-aircraft artillery or mechanical problems. In late February 1945 all three Czechoslovak Squadrons moved to Manston in Kent. A number of sorties carried out during the last months of war are worth recording. On 24th March 1945 the Allied troops carried out an opposed crossing of the Rhine and No.310 Squadron escorted the transport planes and gliders which took part in operation Varsity. The 11th April saw the Czechoslovak Wing escort 129 Halifaxes to the raid on Nürnberg which was tantalisingly close to the Czechoslovakian Border. The last offensive mission, carried out on 25th April 1945 was a raid on coastal batteries on Wangerooge on Ostfriesisch Inseln. The squadron remained at Manston until the end of the war and despite a visit by Air Vice Marshal Karel Janousek to the Supreme Commander, General Dwight Eisenhower, on the 6th May 1945 to gain permission for the Czechoslovak Wing to operate from airfields on Czechoslovakian territory, which had been liberated by the 3rd US Army commanded by General George S. Patton. The pilots wanted to support the uprising in Prague against the remaining German forces, however this request was denied. Nevertheless, some sorties were performed in May, on the 1st a weather reconnaissance made by Flying Officer V. Popelka and Flight Sergeant B. Smid, and on the 12th, No.310 Squadron participated in Operation *Nestegg*, the liberation of the Channel Islands, again without incident.

On 8th May 1945 the radio announced the end of war in Europe. The Czechoslovak pilots hoped for an early return to their country but this did not happen for some time. Instead they continued training exercises, including mock dogfights with other Allied fighters. In the course of one of those combats with American P-51s, over the sea near Suffolk, on 15th June two Spitfires flown by Flying Officer Viktor Popelka and Warrant Officer Jindrich Landsman collided. Popelka survived bailing out and was picked up by the crew of trawler HMS *Florio*. However Landsman's Spitfire crashed

into the sea near Potter Bridge and his body was never found. He was the last of the squadron's pilots to lose his life while serving with the RAF. On 24th June No.310 Squadron and the rest of the Czechoslovak Wing was led by Wing Commander Jaroslav Hlado in a fly-past over North Weald. In July the squadron changed its Spitfire F Mk.IXs for the new LF Mk.IXE and on 7th August Czechoslovak fighter pilots took-off from British soil for the last time. At eight o´clock they departed from Manston airfield with 54 Spitfires all wearing the Czechoslovak insignia. Bad weather forced them to land on airfield R16 at Hildesheim and the weather did not permit them to continue their journey for six days. On 13th August 1945 at 0500 No.310 Squadron landed at Praha-Ruzyne Airport. The pilots, but not all of those who had left their country, had finally returned home after an absence of six years. A month later the squadron moved to Kbely, another of Prague´s airfields. On 16th February 1946, Headquarters RAF officially disbanded No.310 (Czechoslovak) Squadron and in the post-war Czechoslovak Air Force it became the basis of 1.*letecka divize* (1st Air Division) composed of the 10.*stihaci pluk* (10th Fighter Regiment) and 12.*stihaci pluk* (12th Fighter Regiment). But that it is another story.

Manston, spring 1945. The war is over, and the Czechoslovaks are preparing their return home. In the background are some Mosquitoes of No.29 Squadron which were also based at Manston. (V. Kolesa via P. Vancata)

APPENDICES

During the summer of 1940 Hurricanes of No.310 Squadron had the Czechoslovakian national insignia painted on both sides of the cowling, however these soon disappeared and were never replaced by any other insignia. (Via A. Thomas)

No.310 (Czechoslovak) Squadron

Authorized H.M. King George VI : September 1942

CODE : NN

Formed	Disbanded
10.07.40	15.02.46

DESCRIPTION

In front of a sword erect, a lion rampant *queue fourchée*

MOTTO

WE FIGHT TO REBUILD

SIGNIFICANCE OF DESIGN

A lion rampant, *queue fourchée*, argent, forms one of the principle charges in the armorial bearings of Czechoslovakia. The lion gules still rampant - in this badge is indicative of the undefeated Czech peoples in their fight for freedom. The sword erect and unsheathed represents the operational role of fighters.

Jerrard Jefferies-Latimer was the only British officer who served as Flight Leader and CO of No.310 Squadron. He was later killed in the war with Bomber Command.

SQUADRON COMMANDERS

S/L G.D.M. BLACKWOOD*	
	12.07.40 - 01.01.41
S/L J. JEFFERIES-LATIMER*	
	01.01.41 - 07.07.41
S/L F. WEBER	07.07.41 - 07.04.42
S/L F. DOLEZAL	07.04.42 - 15.01.43
S/L E. FOIT	15.01.43 - 13.01.44
S/L H. HRBACEK	13.01.44 - 21.05.44
S/L V. RABA	21.05.44 - 15.09.44
S/L J. HARTMAN	15.09.44 - 13.08.45

*British.

OPERATIONAL DATA

NUMBER OF SORTIES

	Hurr. I	Hurr. II	Spitfire II	Spitfire V	Spitfire VI	Spitfire IX
First sortie	17.08.40	21.03.41	18.11.41	25.11.41	22.07.43	02.03.44
Last sortie	20.03.41	09.12.41	18.11.41	03.02.44	17.09.43	10.07.44
Total 1				5,682		1,306
First sortie				23.07.44		28.08.44
Last sortie				28.08.44		12.05.45
Total 2				45		1,123
Total by type	1,338	1,352	2*	5,727	137	2,429

*One could not be identified, being either a Spitfire II or V.
Total for the unit : 10,985 sorties.

	Hurr. I	Hurr. II	Spitfire II	Spitfire V	Spitfire VI	Spitfire IX
Aircraft lost	17	4	1	22	-	23
Claims (Conf. & Prob.)	49.5	3	-	16.5	-	3
V-1s	-	-	-	-	-	4

Total for the unit : 67 aircraft lost, 72 claims, 4 V-1s.

NUMBER OF PILOTS LOST

	Hurr. I	Hurr. II	Spitfire II	Spitfire V	Spitfire VI	Spitfire IX
Killed	4	2	1	16	-	9
PoW	-	--	-	2	-	2
Evaded	-	-	-	-	-	2

Total for the unit : 32 pilots killed, 4 pilots PoW, 2 evaded.

BREAKDOWN OF PILOTS KILLED BY CITIZENSHIP

British :	1
Czechoslovaks :	30
Pole :	1

DETAILS OF THE FIRST AND LAST MISSION (SERIAL, NAME, TIME OF DEPARTURE AND RETURN)

17.08.40

Sector patrol

R4089/R	F/L J. Jefferies	1410	1455
R4087/X	Sgt J. Hubacek	1410	1455
P3889/S	Sgt J. Rechka	1410	1455
P3142/M	P/O F. Rypl	1410	1455
P3148/N	P/O E. Fechtner	1420	1450

12.05.45

Operation *Nestegg*

MH908/A	F/L K. Drbohlav	0945	1235
MH323/L	F/O F. Chmura	0945	1235
BS409/R	F/Sgt M. Churan	0945	1235
MA803/F	F/O J. Slepica	0945	1235
MH582	F/Sgt J. Chmelik	0945	1235
BS147/E	F/O M.S. Nagy	0945	1235
BS512/U	F/Sgt V. Nedelka	0945	1235
BS249	F/O V. Popelka	0945	1235
BS127	F/Sgt B. Smid	0945	1235
JL227	F/Sgt J. Kravec	0945	1235
MA819/Y	F/Sgt E. Bocek	0945	1235

Major Awards*

DSO	DFC	DFM
NONE	**9**	NONE

DFC : *9*
BAR : NONE

*For security reasons most of the awards received by citizens of occupied Europe were not published in the London Gazette. This was to avoid any kind of vengeance attacks being made on next-of-kin who remained in their homeland.

F/L V. Raba receiving the Czechoslovak War Cross 1939 from the Czechoslovak President Dr. E. Benes. This was the classic award given to members the Czechoslovakian armed forces of WW2. (V. Kolelsa via P. Vancata)

HIGHER COMMANDS

FIGHTER COMMAND
Duxford Sector, No.12 Group
17.08.40/26.06.41

Debden Sector, No.11 Group
26.06.41/20.07.41

Dyce Sector, No.14 Group
20.07.41/24.12.41

Portreath Sector, No.10 Group
24.12.41/08.03.42

Middle Wallop Sector, No.10 Group
08.03.42/21.03.42

Portreath Sector, No.10 Group
21.03.42/07.05.42

Exeter Sector, No.10 Group
07.05.42/16.08.42

Kenley Sector, No.11 Group
16.08.42/21.08.42

Exeter Sector, No.10 Group
21.08.42/26.06.43

Kirkwall Sector, No.14 Group
26.06.43/15.07.43

Kirkwall Sector, No.13 Group
15.07.43/19.09.43

Middle Wallop Sector, No.10 Group
19.09.43/08.11.43

No.134 (Czechoslovak) Airfield, No.84 Group
08.11.43/15.11.43

ADGB
No.134 (Czechoslovak) Airfield, No.84 Group
15.11.43/07.01.44

2ND TACTICAL AIR FORCE
No.134 (Czechoslovak) Airfield, No.84 Group
07.01.44/12.05.44

No.134 (Czechoslovak) Wing, No.84 Group
12.05.44/29.06.44

ADGB/FIGHTER COMMAND
No.134 (Czechoslovak) Wing, No.11 Group
29.06.44/24.08.45

Known individual letters

A : P3707*, R4085*, V7659*, AD365, AR423, AR501, BS472, MA814, MH376, MH908
B : P3069*, V6608*, V7009*, V7588*, AR491, BS141, BS249, EP233, MH839, MJ663
C : P3056*, Z2493*, AR610, BS437, EE635, EE637, EP411, EP453, EP614, MA235, MJ829
D : P3143*, R6770, V6797*, V7597*, W9323*, AD542, AR491, AR502, BR297, BS555, EP452, MA301, MH881, NH179, TE551
E : V6556*, Z2312*, AD574, BL517, BR252, BS147, EE725, EP464, MJ722
F : P8811*, V6642*, Z2393*, AB509, AD328, BS146, BS286, EP413, JL227, MA803, MH843, MH878, MH908, MK228, NH273, TE571
G : N2457*, P2953*, P3539*, V7405*, Z2400*, Z2505*, AD331, AR521, BR577, BS442, MA639, MH355, MK304, TE513
H : V7436*, Z2768*, AB519, AD365, AR468, AR514, BR579
I :
J : V6579*, Z2770*, AD382, AR495, BS248, EE661, EP347, MA477, MK150
K : AB522, AR509, BR304, EP637, LZ920
L : AD378, BL265, MH323
M : P2795*, P3142*, Z2563*, AR491, BL591, BS544, EE485, EP411, LZ916, MH819, MJ906
N : P3148*, Z3400*, AD420, AR462, BM258, MA845, MJ291, NH381, TE565
O : V7304*, Z2643*, BS144, MK116, TE563
P : P3644*, P3887*, P7837, V7412*, AA969, AD366, BS403, EE631, EP127, EP250, MJ605
Q : P3148*, R7298, AD423, AR503, BL851
R : P7989, R4089*, V7010*, AR499, BS409, TE516
S : P2715*, P3889*, V6642*, MK242
T : P8397, P8809*, AD462, AR495, BM400, EE622, MA228, MA229, SL655
U : P3621*, W3575, Z2960*, AD191, AD412, AR499, BL495, BS512, MH330, TE572
V : P7673, V6619*, V7660*, Z2766*, AB212, AB257, BL710, BL767, BM402, EE661, EP364
W : V7008*, AD325, AD468, AD542, AR498, EP250, MJ311, MJ798, NH375
X : L1848*, R4087*, Z3325*, AD325, AD414, BL846, EE746, EN960, EP287, MJ530, TE567
Y : P8814*, R6897, V6643*, AD464, BL497, EE768, MA819
Z : L1842*, AB368, AD422, AR491, AR500, BL923, BS126, EP572, MJ714, MJ829, NH375

*HURRICANE

F/Sgt V. Skreka-Baudoin with a mechanic, in front of his Spitfire IX BS147/NN-E in April 1945 at Manston. (J. Rajlich)

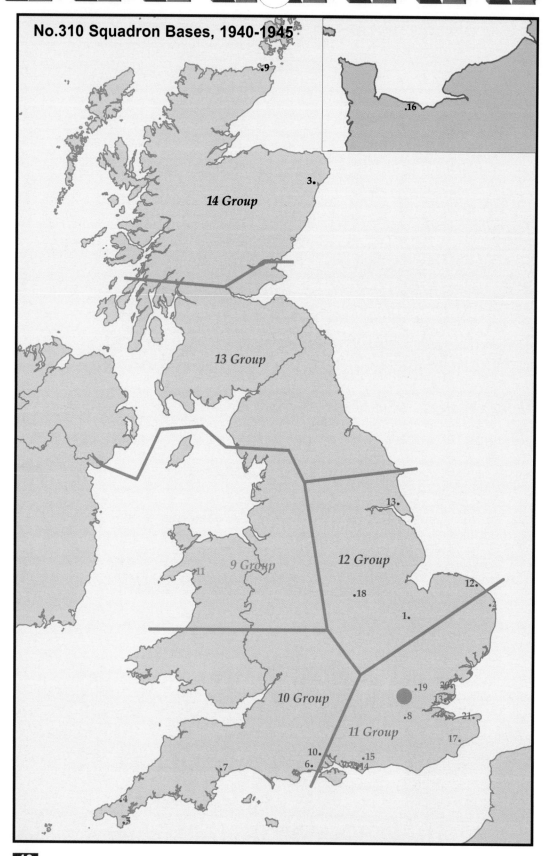

No.310 Squadron Bases, 1940-1945

14 Group

13 Group

9 Group

12 Group

10 Group

11 Group

SQUADRON BASES, UNITED KINGDOM AND CONTINENTAL EUROPE

Duxford [1]	10.07.40 - 26.06.41	Ibsley [10]*	15.12.43 - 19.02.44
Martlesham Heath [2]	26.06.41 - 20.07.41	Mendlesham [12]*	19.02.44 - 21.02.44
Dyce [3]	20.07.41 - 24.12.41	Hutton Cranswick [13]*	21.02.44 - 25.02.44
Perranporth [4]	24.12.41 - 09.02.42	Mendlesham [12]*	25.02.44 - 28.03.44
Predannack [5]	09.02.42 - 11.02.42	Southend [13]*	28.03.44 - 03.04.44
Perranporth [4]	11.02.42 - 08.03.42	Appledram [14]*	03.04.44 - 22.06.44
Warmwell [6]	08.03.42 - 21.03.42	Tangemere [15]*	22.06.44 - 28.06.44
Perranporth [4]	21.03.42 - 07.05.42	B10/Plumetôt*** [16]*	28.06.44 - 29.06.44
Exeter [7]	07.05.42 - 16.08.42	Tangemere [15]	29.06.44 - 01.07.44
Redhill [8]	16.08.42 - 21.08.42	Lympne [17]	01.07.44 - 11.07.44
Exeter [7]	21.08.42 - 26.06.43	Digby [18]	11.07.44 - 28.08.44
Castletown [9]**	26.06.43 - 19.09.43	North Weald [19]	28.08.44 - 29.12.44
Ibsley [10]	19.09.43 - 02.12.43	Bradwell Bay [20]	29.12.44 - 27.02.45
Llanbedr [11]	02.12.43 - 15.12.43	Manston [21]	27.02.45 - 07.08.45

On its way to Prague the unit broke its journey at Hildesheim (R-16), near Hannover, on 07.08.45 and did not continue on to Prague until 13.08.45
* 2 TAF
**Passed from under No.13 Group authority on 15.07.43.
***France

During its defensive period, and due to the limited range of it's interceptors, Fighter Command's squadrons had to be positioned where they could most easily intercept enemy aircraft on their route to their targets. As the most frequent Luftwaffe attacks were directed at south-east England it was in the region controlled by No.11 Group that most aerial activity occurred. The intensity of the fighting on this front made it necessary for squadrons to be changed at regular intervals, to allow operationally tired or lost pilots be replaced so that units could quickly be brought up to strength again. This situation meant that a considerable number of airfields had to be available to the Command. When Fighter Command, and subsequently the 2nd Tactical Air Force, began offensive operations over France, it was necessary, again due to range limitations of its fighters, that they be located as close to enemy forces across the Channel as was practical and thus many temporary airfields proliferated.

Three Spitfires Mk.Vs, on dispersal at Castletown in Scotland during the summer of 1943, awaiting their pilots. (J. Rajlich)

OPERATIONAL DIARY - NUMBER OF SORTIES

DATE	NUMBER						
		07.10.40	1	19.01.41	1	11.04.41	4
		09.10.40	12	*Total for the month : 62*		12.04.41	4
17.08.40	5	10.10.40	16			13.04.41	2
18.08.40	12	11.10.40	12	01.02.41	14	14.04.41	4
19.08.40	8	12.10.40	14	05.02.41	13	16.04.41	2
20.08.40	21	14.10.40	11	11.02.41	14	17.04.41	8
21.08.40	27	16.10.40	3	12.02.41	1	19.04.41	2
22.08.40	1	18.10.40	6	14.02.41	4	20.04.41	14
23.08.40	24	20.10.40	16	16.02.41	2	25.04.41	2
24.08.40	20	25.10.40	13	18.02.41	10	26.04.41	4
25.08.40	13	26.10.40	13	22.02.41	2	27.04.41	4
26.08.40	24	27.10.40	23	23.02.41	11	29.04.41	2
28.08.40	23	28.10.40	15	24.02.41	2	30.04.41	6
29.08.40	11	29.10.40	35	25.02.41	13	*Total for the month : 106*	
30.08.40	24	*Total for the month : 239*		26.02.41	1		
31.08.40	48			28.02.41	2	02.05.41	6
Total for the month : 261		01.11.40	22	*Total for the month : 89*		03.05.41	2
		02.11.40	9			04.05.41	9
01.09.40	6	03.11.40	3	01.03.41	14	06.05.41	2
02.09.40	19	05.11.40	21	02.03.41	12	07.05.41	11
03.09.40	21	07.11.40	11	04.03.41	12	08.05.41	1
04.09.40	12	08.11.40	3	05.03.41	12	09.05.41	2
05.09.40	22	13.11.40	12	06.03.41	1	10.05.41	10
06.09.40	29	15.11.40	8	08.03.41	2	11.05.41	3
07.09.40	24	21.11.40	6	10.03.41	2	12.05.41	4
09.09.40	12	23.11.40	12	12.03.41	3	14.05.41	6
11.09.40	12	24.11.40	3	13.03.41	2	15.05.41	2
14.09.40	24	26.11.40	3	14.03.41	9	16.05.41	12
15.09.40	24	27.11.40	3	16.03.41	4	18.05.41	9
16.09.40	15	28.11.40	3	18.03.41	4	20.05.41	6
17.09.40	12	*Total for the month : 119*		19.03.41	2	21.05.41	6
18.09.40	36			20.03.41	2	22.05.41	6
19.08.40	3	05.12.40	12	21.03.41	1	26.05.41	2
20.09.40	12	06.12.40	2	22.03.41	3	30.05.41	1
21.09.40	10	12.12.40	6	23.03.41	6	*Total for the month : 100*	
23.09.40	24	16.12.40	17	24.03.41	1		
24.09.40	24	24.12.40	9	27.03.41	20	01.06.41	2
25.09.40	12	30.12.40	3	30.03.41	11	03.06.41	2
26.09.40	15	*Total for the month : 49*		31.03.41	8	04.06.41	6
27.09.40	35			*Total for the month : 131*		07.06.41	2
28.09.40	24	01.01.41	3			09.06.41	2
30.09.40	11	03.01.41	3	02.04.41	9	13.06.41	4
Total for the month : 438		05.01.41	18	04.04.41	5	14.06.41	2
		09.01.41	18	07.04.41	2	15.06.41	8
04.10.40	6	11.01.41	2	08.04.41	22	16.06.41	7
05.10.40	36	12.01.41	6	09.04.41	6	17.06.41	4
06.10.40	7	17.01.41	11	10.04.41	4	18.06.41	13

Date		Date		Date		Date	
19.06.41	2	17.08.41	12	14.10.41	3	06.01.42	6
22.06.41	7	18.08.41	6	15.10.41	2	07.01.42	2
25.06.41	2	19.08.41	6	16.10.41	2	08.01.42	14
26.06.41	14	20.08.41	10	17.10.41	6	09.01.42	10
27.06.41	16	21.08.41	4	18.10.41	4	11.01.42	18
28.06.41	10	22.08.41	2	19.10.41	12	12.01.42	10
29.06.41	24	23.08.41	2	20.10.41	2	14.01.42	6
30.06.41	22	24.08.41	6	21.10.41	8	15.01.42	17
Total for the month : **149**		26.08.41	8	22.10.41	6	17.01.42	17
		27.08.41	6	24.10.41	1	18.01.42	8
01.07.41	8	28.08.41	3	25.10.41	6	20.01.42	6
02.07.41	14	29.08.41	1	26.10.41	1	21.01.42	8
03.07.41	19	30.08.41	7	29.10.41	2	22.01.42	2
04.07.41	17	31.08.41	2	31.10.41	8	24.01.42	14
05.07.41	24	*Total for the month* : **184**		*Total for the month* : **107**		26.01.42	16
06.07.71	30					28.01.42	2
07.07.41	40	01.09.41	4	02.11.41	7	31.01.42	20
08.07.41	12	02.09.41	9	03.11.41	3	*Total for the month* : **212**	
09.07.41	20	03.09.41	5	04.11.41	4		
10.07.41	12	04.09.41	5	05.11.41	2	01.02.42	8
11.07.41	24	05.09.41	6	06.11.41	1	02.02.42	2
12.07.41	26	06.09.41	3	08.11.41	4	04.02.42	23
13.07.41	12	07.09.41	9	10.11.41	2	05.02.42	16
14.07.41	14	08.09.41	3	11.11.41	5	06.02.42	16
17.07.41	38	09.09.41	6	14.11.41	2	07.02.42	8
18.07.41	4	10.09.41	11	15.11.41	4	08.02.42	14
19.07.41	12	11.09.41	12	16.11.41	2	10.02.42	5
21.07.41	8	12.09.41	16	24.11.41	2	11.02.42	22
22.07.41	8	13.09.41	10	25.11.41	6	12.02.42	10
23.07.41	5	14.09.41	4	27.11.41	5	13.02.42	6
24.07.41	29	15.09.41	8	30.11.41	2	14.02.42	14
25.07.41	10	16.09.41	8	*Total for the month* : **51**		15.02.42	6
27.07.41	13	17.09.41	11			16.02.42	28
28.07.41	5	18.09.41	12	01.12.41	2	17.02.42	10
29.07.41	3	19.09.41	2	02.12.41	4	18.02.42	10
30.07.41	11	20.09.41	10	03.12.41	4	19.02.42	6
31.07.41	6	21.09.41	6	04.12.41	2	20.02.42	12
Total for the month : **424**		22.09.41	1	06.12.41	1	22.02.42	18
		23.09.41	2	08.12.41	2	*Total for the month* : **234**	
01.08.41	2	24.09.41	2	09.12.41	1		
02.08.41	23	29.09.41	4	10.12.41	10	05.03.42	2
03.08.41	15	30.09.41	8	27.12.41	4	06.03.42	2
04.08.41	2	*Total for the month* : **177**		28.12.41	8	23.03.42	11
05.08.41	9			30.12.41	14	24.03.42	16
06.08.41	5	02.10.41	4	31.12.41	8	25.03.42	8
07.08.41	12	04.10.41	8	*Total for the month* : **60**		26.03.42	18
08.08.41	16	05.10.41	1			27.03.42	12
12.08.41	5	08.10.41	2	01.01.42	4	29.03.42	2
13.08.41	1	09.10.41	3	02.01.42	10	*Total for the month* : **71**	
14.08.41	6	11.10.41	8	03.01.42	4		
15.08.41	8	12.10.41	10	04.01.42	8	01.04.42	30
16.08.41	5	13.10.41	8	05.01.42	10	02.04.42	36

Date	Value	Date	Value	Date	Value	Date	Value
03.04.42	6	01.06.42	19	31.07.42	52	26.09.42	4
04.04.42	10	02.06.42	6	*Total for the month* : **419**		29.09.42	4
05.04.42	30	03.06.42	26			*Total for the month* : **298**	
06.04.42	8	04.06.42	2	01.08.42	20		
07.04.42	14	05.06.42	10	02.08.42	12	01.10.42	14
08.04.42	10	06.06.42	15	03.08.42	24	02.10.42	8
10.04.42	10	07.06.42	18	04.08.42	12	05.10.42	2
12.04.42	8	08.06.42	17	05.08.42	21	08.10.42	4
14.04.42	8	09.06.42	2	06.08.42	24	09.10.42	17
15.04.42	20	10.06.42	24	07.08.42	2	10.10.42	6
16.04.42	28	11.06.42	14	09.08.42	24	11.10.42	12
17.04.42	18	12.06.42	8	10.08.42	6	12.10.42	16
18.04.42	12	13.06.42	6	11.08.42	8	14.10.42	6
20.04.42	2	14.06.42	4	12.08.42	20	15.10.42	18
21.04.42	16	16.06.42	16	13.08.42	30	18.10.42	8
22.04.42	12	17.06.42	2	14.08.42	16	20.10.42	10
23.04.42	10	19.06.42	6	17.08.42	12	21.10.42	12
24.04.42	10	20.06.42	12	18.08.42	13	22.10.42	2
26.04.42	4	21.06.42	4	19.08.42	36	23.10.42	2
27.04.42	7	22.06.42	6	20.08.42	12	24.10.42	9
28.04.42	16	23.06.42	20	22.08.42	16	25.10.42	2
29.04.42	8	24.06.42	10	23.08.42	8	26.10.42	6
30.04.42	25	25.06.42	2	24.08.42	26	27.10.42	16
Total for the month : **358**		26.06.42	6	26.08.42	6	28.10.42	7
		27.06.42	2	27.08.42	8	31.10.42	10
		28.06.42	16	28.08.42	32	*Total for the month* : **187**	
01.05.42	4	29.06.42	14	29.08.42	18		
02.05.42	4	30.06.42	5	30.08.42	10		
03.05.42	9	*Total for the month* : **292**		*Total for the month* : **416**		01.11.42	2
04.05.42	2					02.11.42	18
05.05.42	2	08.07.42	13	01.09.42	12	03.11.42	12
06.05.42	12	09.07.42	18	02.09.42	14	06.11.42	16
07.05.42	20	10.07.42	18	04.09.42	8	07.11.42	22
08.05.42	28	11.07.42	24	05.09.42	10	08.11.42	12
09.05.42	2	12.07.42	16	06.09.42	13	09.11.42	9
10.05.42	4	13.07.42	24	07.09.42	18	10.11.42	2
11.05.42	4	14.07.42	36	08.09.42	24	11.11.42	15
14.05.42	20	15.07.42	8	09.09.42	8	12.11.42	8
16.05.42	14	16.07.42	6	10.09.42	14	13.11.42	4
18.05.42	10	17.07.42	16	11.09.42	16	14.11.42	28
19.05.42	11	18.07.42	4	12.09.42	6	16.11.42	8
20.05.42	2	19.07.42	4	13.09.42	6	17.11.42	12
21.05.42	2	20.07.42	24	14.09.42	6	18.11.42	13
23.05.42	2	21.07.42	20	15.09.42	14	20.11.42	2
24.05.42	9	22.07.42	14	16.09.42	12	22.11.42	13
25.05.42	6	23.07.42	22	17.09.42	16	23.11.42	12
26.05.42	8	24.07.42	8	18.09.42	20	25.11.42	12
27.05.42	20	25.07.42	16	19.09.42	16	27.11.42	6
29.05.42	4	27.07.42	14	21.09.42	9	28.11.42	2
30.05.42	6	28.07.42	28	22.09.42	18	29.11.42	7
31.05.42	19	29.07.42	14	23.09.42	16	30.11.42	6
Total for the month : **224**		30.07.42	20	25.09.42	14	*Total for the month* : **241**	

Date		Date		Date		Date	
01.12.42	2	13.02.43	14	10.04.43	10	12.06.43	17
03.12.42	14	14.02.43	24	11.04.43	20	13.06.43	13
04.12.42	2	15.02.43	24	12.04.43	4	14.06.43	2
05.12.42	6	16.02.43	16	13.04.43	32	20.06.43	22
06.12.42	10	17.02.43	12	14.04.43	17	21.06.43	14
07.12.42	10	18.02.43	6	15.04.43	16	22.06.43	13
09.12.42	4	20.02.43	16	16.04.43	26	23.06.43	13
11.12.42	4	23.02.43	6	17.04.43	16	24.06.43	14
12.12.42	4	24.02.43	14	18.04.43	12	25.06.43	2
13.12.42	12	25.02.43	6	19.04.43	14	27.06.43	4
14.12.42	12	26.02.43	12	20.04.43	23	29.06.43	5
15.12.42	8	27.02.43	12	21.04.43	8	*Total for the month : 200*	
17.12.42	4	28.02.43	19	23.04.43	10		
18.12.42	10	*Total for the month : 207*		24.04.43	16	01.07.43	4
20.12.42	12			25.04.43	6	05.07.43	10
21.12.42	2	01.03.43	4	26.04.43	8	06.07.43	8
22.12.42	2	02.03.43	10	27.04.43	15	07.07.43	2
23.12.42	16	04.03.43	1	28.04.43	15	09.07.43	8
26.12.42	10	05.03.43	4	30.04.43	16	10.07.43	4
29.12.42	8	06.03.43	12	*Total for the month : 429*		12.07.43	10
30.12.42	14	07.03.43	18			13.07.43	2
31.12.42	14	08.03.43	12	02.05.43	12	14.07.43	4
Total for the month : 180		09.03.43	12	03.05.43	14	16.07.43	4
		10.03.43	8	04.05.43	14	17.07.43	2
02.01.43	19	11.03.43	18	05.05.43	16	18.07.43	4
03.01.43	17	12.03.43	20	06.05.43	6	19.07.43	12
04.01.43	16	13.03.43	10	07.05.43	6	20.07.43	2
05.01.43	4	14.03.43	16	09.05.43	4	21.07.43	6
06.01.43	6	15.03.43	18	12.05.43	2	22.07.43	14
07.01.43	10	16.03.43	3	13.05.43	2	23.07.43	2
08.01.43	6	17.03.43	4	14.05.43	26	24.07.43	4
10.01.43	18	18.03.43	6	15.05.43	20	25.07.43	6
14.01.43	4	19.03.43	4	16.05.43	22	27.07.43	18
15.01.43	19	20.03.43	8	17.05.43	16	28.07.43	12
16.01.43	12	21.03.43	4	18.05.43	16	29.07.43	16
21.01.43	12	26.03.43	2	19.05.43	8	30.07.43	2
22.01.43	14	27.03.43	16	21.05.43	11	*Total for the month : 156*	
23.01.43	13	28.03.43	18	23.05.43	14		
26.01.43	19	29.03.43	14	25.05.43	27	02.08.43	2
27.01.43	12	30.03.43	24	27.05.43	6	03.08.43	6
29.01.43	16	31.03.43	16	28.05.43	20	04.08.43	2
Total for the month : 217		*Total for the month : 282*		29.05.43	21	05.08.43	2
				30.05.43	27	06.08.43	2
01.02.43	2	01.04.43	8	31.05.43	12	07.08.43	2
03.02.43	6	02.04.43	24	*Total for the month : 322*		08.08.43	6
05.02.43	4	03.04.43	18			09.08.43	4
07.02.43	4	04.04.43	26	01.06.43	12	10.08.43	6
08.02.43	2	05.04.43	9	03.06.43	22	11.08.43	4
09.02.43	2	06.04.43	18	04.06.43	11	12.08.43	10
10.02.43	2	07.04.43	2	05.06.43	2	13.08.43	2
11.02.43	2	08.04.43	31	06.06.43	32	14.08.43	7
12.02.43	2	09.04.43	9	11.06.43	2	15.08.43	4

Date	Value	Date	Value	Date	Value	Date	Value
16.08.43	8	03.11.43	6	08.04.44	8	21.06.44	11
17.08.43	4	05.11.43	11	11.04.44	2	22.06.44	35
18.08.43	4	06.11.43	4	12.04.44	10	23.06.44	12
19.08.43	6	07.11.43	22	13.04.44	8	24.06.44	36
20.08.43	6	10.11.43	4	15.04.44	2	25.06.44	12
21.08.43	2	11.11.43	12	17.04.44	2	28.06.44	23
22.08.43	1	13.11.43	2	18.04.44	10	29.06.44	11
23.08.43	6	16.11.43	2	19.04.44	12	30.06.44	31
24.08.43	6	24.11.43	4	20.04.44	23	**Total for the month : 646**	
25.08.43	4	25.11.43	22	21.04.44	7		
26.08.43	8	26.11.43	11	23.04.44	23	02.07.44	11
27.08.43	4	29.11.43	7	**Total for the month : 107**		04.07.44	24
28.08.43	6	**Total for the month : 107**				06.07.44	28
30.08.43	4			01.05.44	12	07.07.44	35
31.08.43	6	01.12.43	12	03.05.44	24	08.07.44	3
Total for the month : 134		20.12.43	9	04.05.44	30	09.07.44	20
		21.12.43	12	07.05.44	12	10.07.44	18
02.09.43	6	22.12.43	18	08.05.44	12	23.07.44	2
03.09.43	6	23.12.43	6	09.05.44	24	25.07.44	2
04.09.43	12	24.12.43	12	10.05.44	24	26.07.44	6
06.09.43	4	26.12.43	2	11.05.44	20	28.07.44	2
07.09.43	2	28.12.43	4	12.05.44	24	**Total for the month : 151**	
08.09.43	11	30.12.43	12	15.05.44	11		
09.09.43	2	31.12.43	24	18.05.44	7	03.08.44	6
10.09.43	7	**Total for the month : 111**		19.05.44	15	08.08.44	2
13.09.43	2			20.05.44	23	09.08.44	2
15.09.43	2	01.01.44	12	21.05.44	12	11.08.44	10
16.09.43	6	02.01.44	4	22.05.44	12	18.08.44	2
17.09.43	6	03.01.44	2	24.05.44	24	25.08.44	2
22.09.43	2	04.01.44	22	25.05.44	12	28.08.44	10
23.09.43	16	05.01.44	20	27.05.44	2	31.08.44	12
24.09.43	28	06.01.44	15	28.05.44	23	**Total for the month : 45**	
25.09.43	15	07.01.44	11	29.05.44	12		
27.09.43	24	08.01.44	8	**Total for the month : 335**		01.09.44	32
Total for the month : 151		14.01.44	24			03.09.44	10
		21.01.44	14	02.06.44	12	05.09.44	11
02.10.43	6	23.01.44	12	03.06.44	12	06.09.44	6
03.10.43	10	24.01.44	2	05.06.44	24	09.09.44	24
04.10.43	10	28.01.44	14	06.06.44	48	10.09.44	11
08.10.43	14	29.01.44	11	07.06.44	48	11.09.44	11
09.10.43	9	**Total for the month : 171**		08.06.44	35	12.09.44	21
15.10.43	6			10.06.44	48	13.09.44	25
16.10.43	12	03.02.44	8	11.06.44	24	14.09.44	10
17.10.43	4	**Total for the month : 8**		12.06.44	48	16.09.44	14
18.10.43	8			13.06.44	12	17.09.44	22
22.10.43	12	02.03.44	11	14.06.44	24	18.09.44	11
23.10.43	4	03.03.44	11	15.06.44	24	19.09.44	6
24.10.43	11	04.03.44	9	16.06.44	28	20.09.44	11
25.10.43	8	15.03.44	12	17.06.44	24	23.09.44	11
28.10.43	11	23.03.44	24	18.06.44	24	26.09.44	12
30.10.43	11	26.03.44	12	19.06.44	24	27.09.44	11
Total for the month : 136		**Total for the month : 79**		20.06.44	16		

30.09.44	23	08.11.44	11	01.03.45	12	15.04.45	2
Total for the month : **282**		11.12.44	13	02.03.45	21	18.04.45	11
		23.12.44	12	06.03.45	2	19.04.45	12
03.10.44	12	24.12.44	12	09.03.45	11	21.04.45	2
06.10.44	12	29.12.44	12	11.03.45	9	25.04.45	13
07.10.44	11	31.12.44	12	12.03.45	11	28.04.45	2
12.10.44	11	*Total for the month* : **94**		13.03.45	11	*Total for the month* : **103**	
14.10.44	12			14.03.45	9		
25.10.44	12	05.01.45	11	15.03.45	9	01.05.45	2
28.10.44	24	15.01.45	2	17.03.45	9	12.05.45	11
29.10.44	11	17.01.45	12	19.03.45	13	*Total for the month* : **13**	
Total for the month : **105**		28.01.45	13	20.03.45	11		
		Total for the month : **38**		21.03.45	11	___**GRAND TOTAL** : **10,985**___	
01.11.44	12			22.03.45	12		
02.11.44	11			23.03.45	12	Extracted from ORB	
05.11.44	12	01.02.45	12	24.03.45	12	AIR27/1680-1683.	
06.11.44	9	03.02.45	13	25.03.45	14		
08.11.44	10	06.02.45	13	30.03.45	6		
10.11.44	12	07.02.45	13	31.03.45	12		
18.11.44	10	08.02.45	10	*Total for the month* : **207**			
21.11.44	10	10.02.45	13				
27.11.44	13	14.02.45	11	03.04.45	12		
29.11.44	12	21.02.45	13	04.04.45	11		
30.11.44	12	22.02.45	12	07.04.45	4		
Total for the month : **123**		23.02.45	10	09.04.45	12		
		24.02.45	13	11.04.45	11		
04.12.44	12	27.02.45	12	13.04.45	9		
05.12.44	10	*Total for the month* : **145**		14.04.45	2		

Armourers of No.310 Squadron at Appledram, Spring 1944, loading a 500 lb bomb under the belly of a Spitfire LF IXC, Flight Sergeant M. Moravec is watching from the right. (V. Kolesa via P. Vancata)

Claim list of probable (P) and confirmed (C) kills

Date	Pilot	Type	Serial	Number	Statute
		Hurricane I			
26.08.40	S/L G.D.M. Blackwood	Do215	P3887/P	1	C
	P/O E. Fechtner	Bf110	P3142/M	1	C
	Sgt E.M. Prchal	Do215	P3157	1	C
31.08.40	F/L J. Jefferies	Do215	R4089/R	1	C
	F/L G.L. Sinclair	Do215	R4084	1	C
	P/O E. Fechtner	Do215	P3889/S	1	C
	F/O J.M. Maly	Bf109	V6621	1	C
	P/O S. Zimprich	Bf109	P3156	1	P
	S/L A. Hess	Bf109	P3056/C	1	C
		Do215	P3056/C	1	C
03.09.40	P/O E. Fechtner	Bf110	P3056/C	1	C
	Sgt B. Fürst	Bf110	V6556/E	1	C
	F/L J. Jefferies	Bf110	P3142/M	1	C
	Sgt J. Kominek	Do215	P4085/A	1	P
	Sgt J. Koukal	Bf110	P3148/N	1	C
	F/O J.M. Maly	Bf110	V7436/H	1	P
	F/L G.L. Sinclair	Bf110	P3143/D	1	C
		Do215	P3143/D	1	C
07.09.40	Sgt B. Fürst	Bf109	P3143/D	1	C
		Bf110	P3143/D	1	P
	P/O V. Göth	Bf110	P8814/Y	2	C
	P/O S. Janouch	Bf110	V6556/E	1	C
	P/O S. Zimprich	Bf110	R4087/X	2	P
	F/O J.E. Boulton	He111	P3888	1	C
09.09.40	P/O V. Bergman	Bf110	V7405/G	1	C
	P/O S.B. Fejfar	Bf110	P3143/D	1	C
	Sgt J. Hubacek	Bf110	R4087/X	1	P
	Sgt J. Rechka	Bf110	P2715/S	1	P
	P/O F. Rypl	Bf109	P3142/M	1	P
	F/O J.E. Boulton	Do215	V7412/P[1]	1	C
	P/O S. Zimprich	Do215	V7304/O	1	C
15.09.40	Sgt J. Kominek	Do215	V7304/O	1	C
	F/L J. Jefferies	Do215	R4089/K	0.25	C
	Sgt J. Hubacek		R4087/X	0.25	C
	Sgt J. Kaucky		P3621/U	0.25	C
	Sgt R. Puda		V6619/V	0.25	C
	F/L J. Jefferies	Do215*	R4089/R	0.5	C
	F/L J. Jefferies	Do215*	R4089/R	0.5	C
	P/O S.B. Fejfar	Do17	V6608/B	1	C
	Sgt J. Kaucky	He111*	P3621/U	0.333	C
	Sgt B. Fürst	He111	P3143/D	1	C
	Sgt J. Rechka	He111	P2715/S	1	C
	Sgt E.M. Prchal	He111*	V6556/E	0.5	C
	F/L J. Jefferies	Bf109	R4089/R	1	C

*Shared with other units.

[1] In the ORB, the aircraft F/O Boulton was flying that day is reported to be P3888, but the aircraft is known to have left the unit on 05.09.40 and flew until July 1942 with No.312 Sqn and No.56 OTU before to be lost in an accident. For V7412, it seems that it arrived at Duxford on 02.09.40 and known to have been lost on 09.09.40.

18.09.40	P/O V. Bergman	Do215	V6608/B	1	C
	P/O S.B. Fejfar	Do215	V6579/J	0.333	C
	P/O S. Janouch		V6556/E	0.333	C
	P/O S. Zimprich	Do215	P3621/U	1	P
	P/O E. Fechtner	Do215	P8809/T	1	C
	F/L J. Jefferies	Do215	R4089/R	1	C
	Sgt M. Jiroudek	Do215	V6642/F	0.5	C
	Sgt R. Puda		P3889/S	0.5	C
	Sgt E.M. Prchal	Do215	P3143/D	1	C
27.09.40	Sgt J. Kominek	Bf109	P3889/S	1	C
	P/O E. Fechtner	Do17	P2715/S	1	P

HURRICANE II

09.04.41	S/L J. Jefferies-Latimer	Ju88	Z2693	1	P*
15.05.41	F/L P.B. Davies	Do17	Z2766/V	1	C
13.08.41	F/O V. Bergman	Ju88	Z3400/N	1	P

*At night

SPITFIRE V

28.04.42	F/L E. Foit	Ju88	BL591/M	0.5	C
	F/Sgt F. Vindis		BM258/N	0.5	C
10.06.42	F/Sgt F. Trejtnar	FW190	AD382/J	1	C
	F/Sgt L. Srom	FW190	BL495/U	1	C
	F/Sgt M. Petr	FW190	AD331/G	1	C
	Sgt K. Janata	FW190	AD365/H	1	P
23.06.42	F/L E. Foit	FW190	AD542/D	1	C
12.07.42	Sgt K. Pernica	Ju88	BL579	0.5	C
	F/Sgt L. Srom		BL495/U	0.5	C

A Czechoslovak pilot is ready to start his engine for another patrol. After the Battle of Britain the Czechoslovaks had few opportunities to shoot down enemy aircraft as they were often based far away from any German aerial activity. (IWM HU40541)

19.08.42	S/L F. Dolezal	Do215	EP452/D	1	P
	Sgt V. Popelka	Do215	EP453/C	1	P
	Sgt K. Pernica	Do217	EP461/JR	1	P
28.08.42	S/L F. Dolezal	Bf109	AR495/J	0.5	C
29.01.43	S/L E. Foit	FW190	AR498/W	1	C
	F/Sgt V. Popelka	FW190	AR521/G	1	C
	F/L V. Chocholin	FW190	EP347/J	1	P
24.09.43	F/L V. Chocholin	Bf110	AR335	1	P
27.09.43	F/L K. Drbohlav	FW190	EP250/P	1	P

SPITFIRE IX

08.06.44	F/O O. Smik	FW190	MJ291/N	1	C
17.06.44	F/O O. Smik	FW190	MJ291/N	1	C
		FW190	MJ291/N	0.5	C
	F/O F. Vindis		NH425	0.5	C
08.07.44	*F/O O. Smik*	*V-1*	*EN527*	*3*	*C*
09.07.44	*F/O J. Pipa*	*V-1*	*NH692*	*1*	*C*

SPITFIRE V

| 08.08.44 | F/O S.J.J. Masek | Do217 | AR441 | 0.5 | C |
| | Sgt A. Elbogen | | EN899 | 0.5 | C |

Aircraft damaged : 30

AIRCRAFT LOST ON OPERATIONS

Date	Pilot	Cause	Serial	Mark	Fate
		HURRICANE			
26.08.40	P/O V. Bergman	1	P3960	I	-
	S/L G.D.M. Blackwood	1	P3887/P	I	-
31.08.40	P/O J. Sterbacek	1	P3159	I	†
	P/O M. Krebda	1	P8814/Y	I	-
03.09.40	Sgt J. Kopriva	1	P8811/F	I	-
07.09.40	Sgt J. Koukal	1	V7437	I	-
09.09.40	F/O J.E. Boulton	3	V7412/P[1]	I	†
	F/L G.L. Sinclair	3	R4084	I	-
15.09.40	S/L A. Hess	1	R4085/A	I	-
	Sgt J. Hubacek	1	R4087/X	I	-

Flight Lieutenant J. Maly's Hurricane lying in a field after his aircraft collided, on 29.10.40, with the Hurricane flown by Pilot Officer E. Fechtner who was killed in the accident. (via A. Thomas).

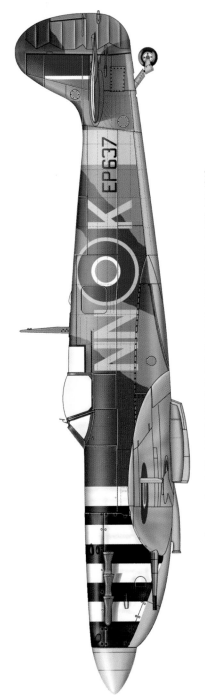

Supermarine Spitfire Mk.VB EP637, No.310 (Czechoslovak) Squadron, Redhill July 1942.
Between 03.07.1942 and 08.07.1942, No.310 Squadron was temporarily detached in Redhill for Operation *Rutter*, the original version of Operation *Jubilee*. For this matter, mechanics painted four white stripes, whose were never used during *Jubilee* on 19.08.1942. When *Rutter* was soon cancelled in the after-noon on 08.07.1942, orders were given to delete those stripes.

27.09.40	F/L G.L. Sinclair	1	V6608/B	I	-
29.10.40	P/O E. Fechtner	3	P3889/S	I	†
01.11.40	Sgt F. Vindis	3	P8809/T	I	-
02.11.40	Sgt J. Kominek	3	L1842/Z	I	-
05.11.40	Sgt M. Jiroudek	3	V7588/B	I	-
	Sgt R. Puda	1	V6619/V	I	-

SPITFIRE

04.02.42	Sgt Z. Skarvada	3	AD412/U	VB	PoW
23.06.42	P/O J. Strihavka	3	BL265/L	VB	-
	P/O F. Trejtnar	1	BL517/E	VB	-
	W/C A. Vasatko	1	BM592/AV	VB	†
31.07.42	F/L B. Kimlicka	3	EP355	VB	-
11.09.42	Sgt K. Janata	3	EP453/C	VB	†
22.09.42	Sgt A. Stanek	2	AR495/T	VC	†
07.11.42	P/O J. Doucha	1	AR502/D	VC	†
29.01.43	W/O J. Sala	1	AB519/H	VB	†
	W/O M. Petr	1	EP464/E	VB	†
27.02.43	F/L F. Burda	1	EP287/X	VB	PoW
	F/L V. Ridkosil	1	EP572/Z	VB	†
28.03.43	F/L H. Hrbacek	3	EE725/E	VC	-
27.04.43	F/O O. Pavlu	2	EE635/C	VC	†
03.05.43	W/O K. Körber	1	EN960/X	VB	†
04.05.43	W/O J. Chlup	3	EP127/P	VB	†
24.09.43	F/L V. Chocholin	1	AR335	VC	†
15.05.44	F/Sgt A. Sveceny	3	MJ509	IX	-
21.05.44	S/L H. Hrbacek	2	MJ798/W	IX	Eva.
	W/O K. Valasek	2	MJ663/B	IX	PoW
	F/Sgt A. Meier	2	MK116/O	IX	†
07.06.44	F/Sgt M. Moravec	3	MJ906/M	IX	†
29.06.44	Sgt J. Bauer	2	NH570	IX	†
11.08.44	Sgt A. Elbogen	3	AR441	VB	†
31.08.44	F/Sgt F. Rehor	3	EN127/P	IX	†
03.09.44	W/O A. Skach	3	MJ311/W	IX	†
05.09.44	F/O R.V. Kanovsky	2	MH616	IX	PoW
	W/O A. Kaminek	2	MA226	IX	Eva.
12.10.44	F/Sgt J. Kauer	3	MH839/B	IX	-
04.12.44	S/L J. Hartman	3	MH843/F	IX	-
23.12.44	F/Sgt J. Kauer	3	MH878/F	IX	†
05.01.45	F/Sgt V. Nikl	3	LZ916/M	IX	-
22.02.45	Sgt J. Chmelik	3	MH376/A	IX	-

Total : 49

1 Enemy aircraft
2 Flak
3 Other causes

[1] In the ORB, the aircraft F/O Boulton was flying that day is reported to be P3888, but the aircraft is known to have left the unit on 05.09.40 and flew until July 1942 with No.312 Sqn and No.56 OTU before to be lost in an accident. For V7412, it seems that it arrived at Duxford on 02.09.40 and known to have been lost on 09.09.40.

AIRCRAFT LOST BY ACCIDENT

Date	Pilot	Duty	Serial	Mark	Fate
		HURRICANE			
16.10.40	Sgt J. Chalupa	Training	P3143/D	I	†
08.06.41	Sgt J. Kominek	Training	Z2562	IIA	†
31.08.41	F/O E. Foit	Training	Z2505/G	IIA	-
24.09.41	Sgt A. Dvorak	Ferry	Z2766/V	IIA	†
24.10.41	F/O E. Nezbeda	Training	Z2493/C	IIA	-
		SPITFIRE			
19.11.41	F/O V. Zaoral	Training	P7837/A	IIA	†
08.12.41	P/O W. Sniechowski	Training	AD468/W	VB	†
14.02.42	F/L M. Kredba	Training	AD414/X	VB	†
12.04.42	F/L S. Zimprich	Training	BL497/Y	VB	†
	Sgt S. Halama	Training	AD420/N	VB	†
26.04.44	P/O V. Lysicky	Training	MK150/J	IX	†
28.10.44	Sgt V. Nikl	Training	MA228/T	IX	-
19.02.45	Sgt J. Jiranek	Training	BS144/O	IX	-
23.02.45	Sgt K. Macura	Training	MA230	IX	†
06.04.45	Sgt S. Zoul	Training	MA845/N	IX	-
02.05.45	F/Sgt M. Kratochvil	Training	LZ920/K	IX	-
15.06.45	W/O J. Landsman	Training (Collided)	MH323/L	IX	†
	F/O V. Popelka	Training (Collided)	MH330/U	IX	-

Total : 18

The remains of Sgt J. Jiranek's Spitfire after his accident of 19th February 1945. He escaped unhurt. (J. Rajlich)

✝

ROLL OF HONOUR-AIRCREW

Name	Service No	Rank	Age	Origin	Date	Serial
BAUER, J.	RAF 788248	Sgt	20	(cz)/RAF	29.06.44	NH570
BOULTON, J.E.	RAF 40362	F/O	21	RAF	09.09.40	V7412
CHALUPA, J.	RAF 787659	Sgt	21	(cz)/RAF	16.10.40	P3143
CHLUP, J.	RAF 787183	W/O	23	(cz)/RAF	04.05.43	EP127
CHOCHOLIN, V.	RAF 81886	F/L	27	(cz)/RAF	24.09.43	AR335
DOUCHA, J.	RAF 117613	P/O	28	(cz)/RAF	07.11.42	AR502
DVORAK, A.	RAF 787672	Sgt	25	(cz)/RAF	24.09.41	Z2766
ELBOGEN, A.	RAF 788096	Sgt	24	(cz)/RAF	11.08.44	AR441
FECHTNER, E.	RAF 81887	P/O	24	(cz)/RAF	29.10.40	P3889
HALAMA, S.	RAF 788017	Sgt	27	(cz)/RAF	12.04.42	AD420
JANATA, K.	RAF 788040	Sgt	24	(cz)/RAF	11.09.42	EP453
KAUER, J.	RAF 787634	F/Sgt	25	(cz)/RAF	23.12.44	MH878
KOMINEK, J	RAF 787980	Sgt	27	(cz)/RAF	08.06.41	Z2562
KÖRBER, K.	RAF 787699	W/O	25	(cz)/RAF	03.05.43	EN960
KREDBA, M.	RAF 81895	F/L	28	(cz)/RAF	14.02.42	AD414
LANDSMAN, J.	RAF 788129	W/O	24	(cz)/RAF	15.06.45	MH323
LYSICKY, V.	RAF 169985	P/O	28	(cz)/RAF	26.04.44	MK150
MACURA, K.	RAF 788497	Sgt	24	(cz)/RAF	23.02.45	MA230
MEIER, A.	RAF 788332	F/Sgt	30	(cz)/RAF	21.05.44	MK116
MORAVEC, M.	RAF 787609	F/Sgt	25	(cz)/RAF	07.06.44	MJ906
PAVLU, O.	RAF 787702	F/O	27	(cz)/RAF	27.04.43	EE635
PETR, M.	RAF 787602	W/O	31	(cz)/RAF	29.01.43	EP464
REHOR, F.	RAF 787229	F/Sgt	24	(cz)/RAF	31.08.44	EN127
RIDKOSIL, V.J.P.	RAF 82944	F/L	28	(cz)/RAF	27.02.43	EP572
SALA, J.	RAF 787450	W/O	28	(cz)/RAF	29.01.43	AB519
SKACH, A.	RAF 788032	W/O	27	(cz)/RAF	03.09.44	MJ311
SNIECHOWSKI, W.	RAF P0321	P/O	24	PAF	08.12.41	AD468
STANEK, A.	RAF 787158	Sgt	22	(cz)/RAF	22.09.42	AR495
STERBACEK, J.	RAF 81901	P/O	27	(cz)/RAF	31.08.40	P3159
VASATKO, A.	RAF 83233	W/C	33	(cz)/RAF	23.06.42	BM592
ZAORAL, V.	RAF 81903	F/O	26	(cz)/RAF	19.11.41	P7837
ZIMPRICH, S.	RAF 81904	F/L	26	(cz)/RAF	12.04.42	BL497

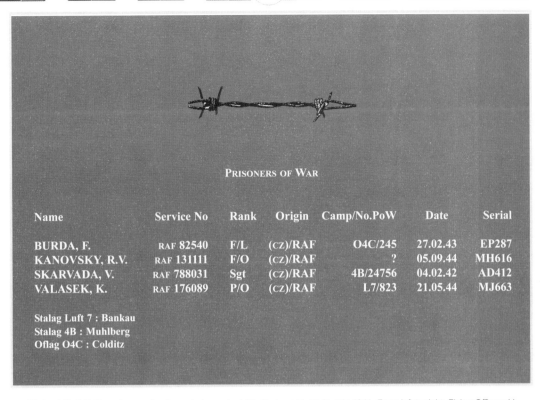

PRISONERS OF WAR

Name	Service No	Rank	Origin	Camp/No.PoW	Date	Serial
BURDA, F.	RAF 82540	F/L	(CZ)/RAF	O4C/245	27.02.43	EP287
KANOVSKY, R.V.	RAF 131111	F/O	(CZ)/RAF	?	05.09.44	MH616
SKARVADA, V.	RAF 788031	Sgt	(CZ)/RAF	4B/24756	04.02.42	AD412
VALASEK, K.	RAF 176089	P/O	(CZ)/RAF	L7/823	21.05.44	MJ663

Stalag Luft 7 : Bankau
Stalag 4B : Muhlberg
Oflag O4C : Colditz

Pilots of No.310 Squadron posing for a photograph at Martlesham Heath in July 1941. From left to right, Flying Officers V. Chocholin, S. Zimprich, J. Hybler, Squadron Leader F. Weber, Flight Lieutenant P.B.G. Davies, Sergeant J. Skirka, Flight Lieutenant M. Kredba, Sergeant M. Jiroudek, Flying Officer E. Nezbeda. Sitting in the front is Pilot Officer B. Kimlicka. Three of these, V. Chocholin, S. Zimprich and M. Kredba, were to lose their lives while serving with the squadron. All the others survived the war including P.B.G. Davies who became a PoW while serving with No.611 Squadron. (IWM HU40527)

Squadron founder members, Duxford on 19th July 1940.
Sitting L-R: P/O F. Rypl, F/O J. E. Boulton, P/O J. Ambrus, S/L G. D. M. Blackwood, W/C A. B. Woodhall, P/O A. Hess, F/L G. L. Sinclair, P/O J. M. Maly, F/O L. C. Czesek (interpreter, Briton of Czech origin), Standing L-R: P/O J. Himr, P/O M. Kredba, P/O K. Vykoukal, P/O F. Hradil, P/O E. Fechtner, P/O V. Chocholin, P/O J. Polivka (technical officer), P/O V. Göth, P/O J. Sterbacek, P/O V. Zaoral, P/O R. Rohacek, P/O R. Holecek, P/O A. Navratil, P/O S. Janouch, P/O F. Kordula a P/O S. Zimprich. (J. Rajlich)

SQUADRON ROSTER

NAME	RANK[1]	STATUS

*Flight Leader, ** Squadron Leader, ***Flight Leader/Squadron Leader
@ Pilots at the Squadron in August 1945.
(†) Pilots killed serving with Squadron.

AMBRUS, Jan P/O (CZ)/RAF
7-40/8-40[2] RAF No.81883
Slovak[3]. Prewar CzAF fighter pilot in Air Regiment 6. With FAF 1939-1940 serving in EC Chartres before escaping to the UK. Posted to No.310 Sqn as reserve pilot, but did not fly, having to be trained on Hurricane. Posted to No.6 OTU. First CO No.312 (Czech) Sqn September - December 1940. Withdrawn from operational duty due of his age, 41 in 1940. Air Attache in Canada until the end of the war. Returned to Czechoslovakia in 1945, but emigrated to Canada after the Communist coup in 1948. He was the only Slovak fighter pilot of the Battle of Britain.

BAUER, Jiri Sgt (CZ)/RAF
6-44/6-44 (†) RAF No.788248
Fresh graduate, posted from No.84 GSU. Transferred from Cz Army in March 1942.

BERGMAN, Vaclav* P/O (CZ)/RAF
7-40/1-43 RAF No.81884
See biography. A flight CO between 07.04.42 and 01.10.42, succeeding F. Dolezal. Replaced by V. Chocholin. **DFC** [No.19 Sector HQ].
F/O : 2-41, F/L : 1-42

BERNARD, Frantisek* Sgt (CZ)/RAF
8-40/8-40, 5-44/5-45 RAF No.787543[4]
RAF No.120209
Prewar CzAF member. With FAF 1939-1940 serving with GC II/2 on Moranes before escaping to the UK.

Vaclav BERGMAN
RAF No.81884

Vaclav Bergman was born in Domousice, in the district of Louny, on 27th August 1915, in what was to become Czechoslovakia. In 1935, having completed his studies at Rakovnik Grammar School, he joined the Czechoslovakian Air Force on 1st October and on 1st July 1936 he was posted to the 4. *pozorovaci letka* (Observation Flight) of the 1st Air Regiment at Cheb as an observer. Having decided on a military career he commenced studying at the Military Academy in Hranice na Morave on 1st October 1936 and graduated on 29th August 1937 as a *porucik* (Lieutenant). Completing training as a fighter pilot in July 1938, he was posted to 43. *stihaci letka* (Fighter Flight) of the 4th Air Regiment at Prague - Kbely airfield, flying Avia B-534s. After 15th March 1939 he was demobilised and started work at the Avia aircraft manufacturing company in Prague - Letnany. However, on 17th June 1939 he escaped to Poland, and reached France the following month. Completing a retraining course on French fighters he served during May and June 1940 as a *Lieutenant* with the *Escadrille Légère de Défence* at Chartres, which was flying MS 406s. After the fall of France he escaped to the United Kingdom via Bordeaux.

He joined the RAF as a Pilot Officer on 12th July and was posted to No.310 (Czechoslovak) Squadron. During the unit's first day of operations, 26th August, his aircraft was badly damaged however, despite his wounds, he managed to bale out. During the Battle of Britain he shot down two enemy aircraft. The first, a Bf110, on 9th September and a Do17 on 18th September. On 28th October he shared a damaged Ju88 with two other pilots but had to wait a year before scoring again.

On 13th August 1941 he attacked another Ju88 which was credited as a probable. He became a flight commander in April 1942, damaged a FW190 on 5th June and completed his tour early in October. On 1st January 1943 he joined No.313 (Czechoslovak) Squadron as its B Flight commander and retained this post until September 1943. He then served at the Czechoslovak Inspectorate General in London until 31st January 1944, when he returned to No.313 Squadron to take command the unit. On 22nd May 1944, he was posted to No.19 Sector of 2nd TAF with the rank Wing Commander and on 3rd July was awarded a DFC. Among the many awards he received were the Czech Military Cross 1939 four times. Between February 1945 and June 1945 he was at the Command & General Staff School at Fort Leavenworth (USA) and on returning to London in August he was posted to the RAF Staff College.

He returned to Czechoslovakia in March 1946, and took command of Air Regiment 5 (Fighter), but was then posted to the Staff of the CzAF on 15th April. Following the Communist coup in 1948 he was posted, on 15th March, to command *Letecky pluk* 41 but was then dismissed from the service by the new regime on 1st June 1948. In September he fled to the UK for the second time in his life and in 1949 he rejoined the RAF and was retrained as a flying boat pilot and posted to No.209 Squadron to fly Sunderlands. With this unit he served in Malaya and in Korea, twice commanding a detachment of the squadron at Iwakuni, Japan. He was Mentioned in Despatches on 21st March 1952 and received a BAR to his DFC on 24th April 1953. In 1955 he converted to the Avro Shackleton, but in 1957 he ceased flying duties.

G.D.M.BLACKWOOD

Posted to No.6 OTU for further training. No.601 Sqn September - October 1940, No.238 Sqn October 1940 - April 1941, No.32 Sqn April - December 1941. Second tour of operational duty with No.313 (Czech) Sqn August 1942 - June 1943, then a third tour with the same unit before being posted as Flight Lieutenant to No.310 (Czech) Sqn as last B Flight Commander from 22.05.44 to 13.08.45 replacing V. Raba. Transferred to the new CzAF after 1945, but left Czechoslovakia after the Communist coup of 1948 returning to the UK, serving again with RAF till 1964.

BLACKWOOD, George D.M.** S/L   RAF
7-40/1-41   RAF No.32181
Scot. Posted from No.213 Sqn. Prewar RAF in SSC service ended in April 1938. Recalled for active service in September 1939 as flight instructor. No.213 Sqn May - July 1940 as supernumerary Flight Lieutenant. First British CO No.310 (Czech) Sqn. Posted to HQ No.12 Group (Fighter Command) in January 1941. No more operational posting until the end of war. In 1944, returned with the Czechoslovaks, helping in forming No.134 (Czechoslovak) Wing formed with the three Czech fighter Squadrons, in preparation of Normandy landings. One confirmed victory with No.310 Sqn, Battle of Britain, 1940.

BOCEK, Emil   Sgt   (CZ)/RAF
10-44/8-45@   RAF No.787719
Fresh graduate. Former mechanic with RAF.
F/Sgt : 3-45

BODIE, Crelin A.W.*   F/L   RAF
3-41/6-41   RAF No.42790
Known as "*Bogle*". Posted from No.66 Sqn. Enlisted in RAF just before the war. No.66 Sqn May 1940 - March 1941. B Flight Commander succeeding M.W.B. Knight on 08.03.41. Posted to No.152 Sqn on 03.06.41, replaced by M. Kredba. Five confirmed and six shared victories with No.66 Sqn all during the Battle of Britain. DFC [No.66 Sqn].
†24.02.42, Spitfire IIA P8077, No.152 Sqn, UK.

BOROVEC, Rudolf   P/O   (CZ)/RAF
8-40/9-40, 4-42/10-43   RAF No.81885
Prewar CzAF observer. In Summer 1939 escaped to France via Poland. Trained as pilot in FAF then escaped to the UK. Posted to No.310 Sqn as reserve pilot before being sent to No.6 OTU to be trained on Hurricanes. No.601 Sqn February - June 1941, No.19 Sqn January - April 1942 before being back to No.310 Sqn in April 1942 as Flying Officer. End of tour of operations, October 1943. Volunteered for Czechoslovak air unit on the Eastern Front in Soviet Union. Discharged RAF 31.01.44, sailing the following month. Became a founder member of 1st Cz Fighter Regiment and took part in Slovak National Uprising in October 1944. After the repress of the uprising, he was unable to fly back to Soviet Union because of lack of aircraft, joining the Partisans.
F/O : 4-42
†09.11.44 during ground battle with German army in Slovakian mountains.

J.BRYKS

BOULTON, John E. P/O RAF
7-40/9-40 (†) RAF No.40362
Prewar RAF pilot with a SSC. Flight instructor at the outbreak of war until to be posted to No.310 Sqn. Two confirmed victories with No.310 Sqn, Battle of Britain, 1940.
F/O : 8-40

BRAZDA, Bohuslav Sgt (CZ)/RAF
11-44/8-45@ RAF No.788200
Posted from No.57 OTU. Czech but born in Italy.
F/Sgt : 5-45

BREZOVSKY, Frantisek Sgt (CZ)/RAF
10-40/3-41 RAF No.787664
Posted from No.85 Sqn. Under training with FAF at the EC Chartres 1939-1940 but saw no action. Served shortly with No.85 Sqn in October 1940. No more details except that he served in 1944 with No.291 Sqn.

BRYKS, Josef P/O (CZ)/RAF
7-40/8-40 RAF No. 82538
Prewar CzAF fighter pilot in Air Regiment 2. With Czech Depot at Agde in France 1939-40 but saw no action. Escaped to the UK, then No.310 Sqn. Posted to No.6 OTU for retraining in August 1940. No operational posting before April 1941 (passing through HQ FPP, No.8 MU). No.242 (Canadian) Sqn April - June 1941. Shot down on 17.06.41 and made PoW. Liberated on 16.04.45. Transferred to the new CzAF after 1945 as instructor, but after Communist coup in 1948 was arrested for "planning of escape" and was put into prison for ten years. He tried to escape again but the plan was revealed and he was sentenced for twenty years. He was sent to a communist forced labour camp and on 11.08.57 died on heart stroke in uranic mine "Rovnost". MBE on 09.08.46.

BURDA, Frantisek* P/O (CZ)/RAF
10-40/8-42, 11-42/2-43, 6-45/8-45@ RAF No.82540
Posted from No.6 OTU. Prewar CzAF fighter pilot in Air Regiment 4. With FAF 1939 - 1940 flying with GC I/4 on Curtisses. One confirmed and one shared confirmed victory with the French 1940. Tour expired in August 1942. Returned to operations in November 1942 as B Flight CO from 15.11.42 succeeding E. Foit. Replaced by J. Hartman on 27.02.43

F. BURDA

after being shot down over Brest (France). He bailed out and was captured. Ended as PoW at Oflag O4C at Colditz. Liberated on 16.04.45. Returned to No.310 Sqn in June 1945.
F/O : 3-41, F/L : 8-42

CERMAK, Josef F/Sgt (CZ)/RAF
9-44/8-45@ RAF No.787363
Posted from No.313 (Czech) Sqn. Prewar sport pilot. With Czech Depot at Agde in France 1939-40, then escaped to the UK. After completing his pilot training in GB posted to No.312 (Czech) Sqn October 1943 - May 1944, No.118 Sqn May - July1944, then No.313 (Czech) Sqn July - September 1944.

CERVENY, Frantisek Sgt (CZ)/RAF
10-43/10-44 RAF No. 788111
Fresh graduate. Prewar pilot. With Polish Air Force in 1939. Arrived to GB from internment in Soviet Union in July 1941. Selected for a pilot course in March 1942, after completing pilot training posted to No.310 Sqn in October 1943. Tour expired October 1944.
W/O : 8-44

J. CERMAK

CHALOUPKA, Cenek　　　W/O　　(cz)/RAF
6-45/8-45@　　　　　　　　RAF No. 787656
After retraining posted to No.43 Sqn in July -
September 1941, No.615 Sqn September 1941
onwards. On 06.10.41 shot down by *flak* and made
PoW. Liberated on 16.04.45. Return to GB then, he
was posted to No.310 Sqn for the flight to
Czechoslovakia. Transferred to the new CzAF after
war but died in an flying accident in an Ar96 on
25.02.46.

CHALUPA, Jan　　　　　Sgt　　(cz)/RAF
10-40/10-40 (†)　　　　　　RAF No.787659
Posted from No.6 OTU. Prewar CzAF member under
training as fighter pilot.

CHLUP, Jaroslav　　　　Sgt　　(cz)/RAF
7-41/5-43 (†)　　　　　　　RAF No.787183
Posted from No.52 OTU. Prewar CzAF fighter pilot.
With FAF 1939-1940, known posting with GBA II/35 in
June 1940 then to GB. Retrained and posted to No.24
Sqn in 1940-41. Retrained as fighter pilot in June 1941.
F/Sgt : 10-42, W/O : 3-43

CHMELIK, Jaroslav　　　Sgt　　(cz)/RAF
11-44/8-45@　　　　　　　RAF No. 788427
Fresh graduate, posted from No.57 OTU. Belonging
to No.11 Cz Infantry Battalion in the Middle East.
Volunteered for RAF service in 1942 and accepted for
a pilot training course.
F/Sgt : 4-45

CHMURA, Frantisek　　　F/O　　(cz)/RAF
10-44/8-45@　　　　　　　RAF No.154598
Fresh graduate. Slovak. Performed 34 sorties as air
gunner with No.311 (Czech) Sqn on Wellington from
December 1940 - September 1941. Selected for a
pilot course in 1942 then posted to No.310 Sqn after
completing his course.

J. CHALOUPKA

J. CHMELIK

CHOCHOLIN, Vladislav*   P/O   (CZ)/RAF
7-40/9-40, 9-40/1-43, 6-43/9-43 (†)   RAF No.81886
Known as "*Chocho*". Prewar CzAF fighter pilot in
Air Regiment 6. With FAF 1939-1940 serving in
Chartres before escaping to the UK. Became founder
member of No. 310 Sqn in July 1940. Served briefly
with No.312 (Czech) Sqn in September 1940 before
being posted back to No.310 Sqn. A Flight CO from
01.10.42 succeeding V. Bergman, replaced by H.
Hrbacek on 01.02.43. Rested from February to June
1943. Became B Flight CO of No. 310 Sqn on
01.06.43 replacing J. Hartman when started a second
tour. Replaced by B. Kimlicka on 24.09.43 after his
death.
F/O : 7-41, F/L : 10-42

CHURAN, Miroslav   Sgt   (CZ)/RAF
10-44/8-45@   RAF No.788329
Fresh graduate. No more details available.
F/Sgt : 2-45

CUKR, Vaclav   Sgt   (CZ)/RAF
8-40/8-40   RAF No.787625
Czech. Prewar CzAF fighter pilot in Air Regiment 6.
Later with FAF serving with GC II/3 1939-1940
flying Dewoitines. Two confirmed and four shared
confirmed victories with the French, 1940 then to GB.
Posted to No.6 OTU for retraining, then served briefly with No.43 Sqn in September 1940, No.253 Sqn
September 1940 - May 1941. Later commissioned
and instructor and test pilot, but on 04.07.43 while
serving as test pilot at No.20 MU collided his
Mustang I AG489 in flight with Spitfire IIA P7918
from No.52 OTU. He managed to bail out but too low
and suffered serious injuries. He became invalid and
was not able to fly afterwards. After the war, he returned to Czechoslovakia, and after Communist coup in
1948 emigrated again and in the 1950s joined
Czechoslovak Intellingence Office (CIO). In the
1960s he finally settled down in New Zealand with a
new name of Cooper.

DAVIES, Patrick B.G.*   F/L   (RH)/RAF
12-40/8-41   RAF No.85937
Posted from No.19 Sqn to become A Flight CO succeeding G.L. Sinclair from 12.12.40. Replaced by F.
Dolezal on 29.08.41. Posted to No.19 Sqn. CO No.19
Sqn March 1942 - September 1942. Second tour of
operations during Summer 1943 and posted as super-

V. CHOCHOLIN

numerary Squadron Leader to No.611 Sqn pending
appointement. Shot down and made PoW on 23.08.43.
At least two confirmed victories with Nos.19 and 310
Sqns, Europe 1941-1942. DFC [No.19 Sqn].

DIVIS, Miroslav*   F/L   (CZ)/RAF
7-43/1-45   RAF No.82592
Posted from No.61 OTU. Prewar CzAF observer, then
serving with FAF at Tours. UK in Summer 1940.
No.311 (Czech) Bomber Sqn February 1941 - January
1942, ending his tour with 34 sorties. Retrained as
fighter pilot and posted to No.310 Sqn in July 1943.
Tour expired in January 1945. A flight leader from
11.08.44 and 06.01.45, succeeding J. Hartman.
Replaced by K. Drbohlav.

DOLEZAL, Frantisek***   P/O   (CZ)/RAF
8-40/8-40, 10-40/1-43   RAF No.82593
See biography. A flight commander between 29.08.41
and 07.04.42 replacing P. Davies. When he took command of the Squadron, he relinquished his command
to V. Bergman.
F/L : 1-41, S/L : 4-42

DFC : 10.09.42

Frantisek DOLEZAL
RAF No.82593

Frantisek Dolezal was born in Ceska Trebova on 14th September 1909, the son of an engine-driver. When he finished grammar school in 1928 he went to Prague to study in the Faculty of Machine Engineering at the Czech Institute of Technology. In 1933 the Army called him up for military service and in the course of his training at Josefov he qualified as a Reserve officer and was promoted to the rank of *podporucik* (2nd Lieutenant) in the artillery. In 1934 "Dolly" Dolezal chose a military career and joined the Czech Air Force. He then went to the Air Department's Military Academy at Hranice na Morave and finished, in 1936, at the top of his class and graduated as a *porucik* (1st Lieutenant). In 1937 he completed further training and gained his wings and qualification as an observer. Subsequently he served in the 36.*stihaci letka* (Fighter Flight) of Air Regiment No.2 where he flew Avia B-534s, and during the Munich crisis he performed the duties of a First Officer. After the German occupation of his country he escaped to Poland on 20th June 1939 and on 25th July he sailed from Gdynia for France. He entered the *Armée de l'Air* on 10th October, retrained on French fighters at the CIC in Chartres and on 17th May 1940 he was posted to *Groupe de Chasse* II/2. This unit flew Morane 406s during the fighting in the spring of 1940 and Dolezal claimed one solo, and two shared confirmed victories, and one probable. His first victim was a Bf110 probably destroyed on 21st May which was shared with two French pilots. In the afternoon of 1st June six MS 406s took off from the airfield Chissey against a formation of He111s and he destroyed one of these aircraft. A week later his next victim, a Hs126, was shared with two French pilots. On 15th June, nine pilots of GC II/2 including Dolezal, shot down a Do17 but next day the unit was forced to withdraw to the south. After the fall of France he decided to escape to the United Kingdom and on 24th

June he sailed to North Africa, then from Casablanca to Gibraltar and eventually to Liverpool. In August 1940, he was commissioned into the RAF and posted, on 6th August, to No.310 (Czechoslovak) Squadron. Three weeks later, on 26th August, however, he was attached to No.19 Squadron where he achieved several successes before he wounded in the leg. On 5th September he claimed a Bf109 as probably destroyed, and two days later he destroyed a Bf110 and damaged a He111. On 11th September another Bf109 was credited as probable, however he was again wounded and his Spitfire very badly damaged. A week later he shot down a Ju88. On his return to No.310 Squadron, on 29th October 1940, he became the leader of A Flight. From January 1942 he temporarily led the squadron before being appointed, in April 1942, to command the unit. He led the unit during Operation Jubilee, claiming one Do217 as a probable, one FW190 damaged and, for his services to date he was awarded the DFC. In January 1943 he was promoted to lead the Czechoslovak Wing. He finished his second operational tour on 1st February 1944 and was awarded the DSO and subsequently served at the Czechoslovak Inspectorate General in London. In August 1944 was posted to the United States to study at the Command and General Staff School in Fort Leavenworth, Kansas. He left the RAF on 3rd March 1945 to join the reformed Czechoslovak Forces and returned to his own country at the end of the war with the rank of *podplukovnik* (Lieutenant Colonel). Dolezal did not long survive his return as he was killed in a flying accident on 4th October 1945 when a Si204, in which he was a passenger, crashed near Bucovice na Morave due mainly to bad weather. In addition to his British awards he also received the Czechoslovak Military Cross, four times, Medal for Bravery, three times, and French *Croix de Guerre*.

J. DOUCHA

DOUCHA, Jan P/O (CZ)/RAF
6-42/11-42 (†) RAF No.117613
Posted from No.52 OTU. Czech, born in Austria. Prewar CzAF fighter pilot. Served with the FAF in 1940 with ELD Chateaudun and GC II/2 on Moranes. One confirmed victory with FAF. Evacuated to the UK in Summer 1940, flight instructor in the RAF in 1940, then No.501 Sqn April - May 1941, then OTU again.

DRBOHLAV, Karel* P/O (CZ)/RAF
7-40/7-40, 10-42/7-44, 1-45/8-45@ RAF No. 81906
Posted from Czech Inspectorate. Prewar sport pilot. Trained as fighter pilot in FAF 1939-40 but did not see any action before to be evacuated to the UK. Posted for retraining on Hurricanes to No.6 OTU. No.601 Sqn November 1940 - June 1941, No.313 (Czech) Sqn June - October 1941, and April - May 1942. Second tour of operations from October 1942 with No.310 Sqn and in January 1945 posted to No.310 Sqn from CIG. Tour completed in July 1944, started the next one in January 1945 and became the last A Flight CO from 06.01.45, succeeding M. Divis.
F/L : 4-43

DVORAK, Alois Sgt (CZ)/RAF
10-40/9-41 (†) RAF No.787672
Posted from No.6 OTU. Prewar CzAF fighter pilot in Air Regiment 2. Posted to No.257 Sqn, then returned to No.310 Sqn.

DYGRYN, Josef D. Sgt (CZ)/RAF
9-41/5-42 RAF No.787678
Posted from No.1 Sqn. Also known under the name of Dygryn-Ligoticky. Under training at Flying School in Prostejov in 1938. Served with the FAF in 1939-40 in Avord then escaped to GB. Briefly served with No.85 Sqn October 1940 then posted to No.1 Sqn October 1940 - September 1941. Posted back to No.1 Sqn in May 1942. Five confirmed victories including three at night on Hurricanes, No.1 Sqn, Europe, 1941. DFM [No.1 Sqn].
W/O : 4-42
†04.06.42 Hurricane IIB Z3183, No.1 Sqn, France.

ELBOGEN, Arnost Sgt (CZ)/RAF
5-44/8-44 (†) RAF No.788096
Fresh graduate posted from No.84 GSU. Posted to No.312 Sqn in July 1941 as ground staff member, later selected for a pilot course, being posted to No.310 Sqn after the completion of his course.

FAJTL, Frantisek P/O (CZ)/RAF
8-40/8-40 RAF No.82544
Prewar CzAF fighter pilot in Air Regiment 2. With FAF 1939-1940 serving with ELD Chartres, GC III/9 on Blochs, III/7 and I/6 on Moranes then went to GB. Posted to No.6 OTU for retraining. Later served at No.1 Sqn September 1940, No.17 Sqn September 1940

K. DRBOHLAV

- May 1941. In May 1941 posted to newly created No.313 (Czech) Sqn becoming A flight leader in December. In April 1942 he became the first Czechoslovak to be appointed as CO of a British-manned unit, No.122 Sqn. Shot down in May 1942 but evaded capture, returning to the UK in August. Returned to operations with No.313 Sqn as CO in September 1943. Discharged RAF 31.01.44 to take command of the 1st Cz Fighter Regiment in Soviet Union. One confirmed and three shared victories with Nos.17, 122 and 313 Sqns, Europe, 1940-1942. Remained with the CzAF after the war, he was arrested and dismissed from the service, and later put into jail until July 1951, being partially rehabilitated in 1964. DFC [No.122 Sqn].

FECHTNER, Emil P/O (CZ)/RAF
7-40/10-40 (†) RAF No.81887
See biography.
DFC : 04.11.40

FEJFAR, Stanislav B. P/O (CZ)/RAF
8-40/11-40 RAF No.82545
Prewar CzAF fighter pilot in Air Regiment 3. Escaped to France via Poland in July 1939. Served with the FAF with GC I/6 on Moranes, claiming two confir-

med and one shared victory. Reached UK in July 1940 and posted to No.310 Sqn, pending his training on Hurricane he completed in September when he became operational. Rested from November 1940. Another tour of operations with No.313 (Czech) Sqn July 1941 - May 1942. Five confirmed and two shared confirmed victories with FAF, No.310 and 313 Sqn, Europe, 1940 - 1942.
†17.05.42, Spitfire VB BL973, No.313 (Czech) Sqn, France.

FOIT, Emil A.*** P/O (CZ)/RAF
10-40/11-42, 1-43/1-44 RAF No.83225
See biography. B Flight leader between 14.02.42 and 15.11.42, succeeding M. Kredba. Replaced by F. Burda.
F/O : 2-41, F/L : 2-42, S/L : 1-43
DFC : 08.01.45

FORNUSEK, Adolf W/O (CZ)/RAF
7-42/11-43, 6-44/8-44, 9-44/7-45 RAF No.788015
RAF No.159217
Posted from No.51 OTU. Prewar CzAF fighter pilot in Air Regiment 1. Joined Polish air force in 1939 and retreated to Soviet Union. He sailed to the UK in

B.FÜRST

33

Emil FECHTNER
RAF No.81887

Emil Fechtner was born in Prague on 16th September 1916. He spent his youth in Hradec Kralove where his father worked as an engineer at the Skoda Works. In June 1933 he finished his grammar school studies and began work as a clerk. In 1935 he was called up for military service and posted to Artillery Regiment 104 in Olomouc. During his service in the army he studied to become a Reserve officer and was promoted to the rank of *podporucik* (2nd Lieutenant) in the artillery. Deciding on a military career he entered the Military Academy in Hranice na Morave in 1936 and the following year he transferred to the Air Force and graduated with the rank of *porucik* (1st Lieutenant). Fechtner was subsequently posted to *Stíhaci letka* 38 (Fighter Flight No.38) of *Letecky pluk* 3 (Air Regiment No.3). In October 1937 he was sent at Prostejov for flying training and received his wings in July 1938. During the mobilisation of the Czechoslovak forces in September 1938 he served with *Stíhaci letka* 38 which was operating B-534s, however on 14th March 1939, when the Slovakian State was formed, he returned to Bohemia. On 19th June he escaped to Poland and then to France where he arrived on 1st August. Soon afterwards he joined the French *Armée de l'Air* and was retrained on French aircraft at Chartres and Tarbes but failed to reach an operational unit before the fighting ceased. After the Armistice, in June 1940, he made his way to the United Kingdom and arrived in Falmouth on the 21st. There he joined the RAF and on 12th July 1940 he was posted to No.310 (Czechoslovak) Squadron with

the rank of Pilot Officer. He claimed a number of successes during the summer of 1940 while flying with this unit and took part in the squadron's first combat on 26th August in which he shot down a Bf110. A Do17Z followed on the 31st August and three days later he shot down another Bf110. His last kill was achieved on 18th September when he destroyed a Ju88. In addition to these confirmed kills he claimed a probable victory, a Do17, on 27th September and damaged another Bf110 on 7th September. With four enemy planes destroyed he was the most successful Czechoslovak pilot in No.310 Squadron and was second only to Squadron Leader Gordon Sinclair (RAF). He was awarded the DFC in October. His own country awarded him the Czechoslovak Military Cross and Medal for Bravery. On the 29th of that month he was killed in an accident while flying a Hurricane, and was buried in Roystone cemetery on the 2nd November.

Emil A. FOIT
RAF No.83225

Born in Brno, on 12th March 1913, Emil Foit studied at the Military Academy in Hranice na Morave between 1935 and 1937 and joined the Czechoslovak Air Force on completion of his training. During 1938 he served in Air Regiment 4 as a *porucik* (1st Lieutenant), but was demobilised on 17th March 1939 following the German occupation of Czechoslovakia. He fled to Poland on 7th May 1939 and from there went to France, where he enlisted the French Foreign Legion as a Sergeant. On the outbreak of war he was commissioned into the *Armée de l'Air*. Foit was retrained on French aircraft at Blida in North Africa and then on fighters in Oran (Algeria). On 9th November 1939 he was posted to GC I/9 in North Africa as a *Lieutenant* and flew MS 406s until the Armistice. In June 1940 he was again forced to flee, this time to the United Kingdom where, after receiving training at No.6 OTU, he joined No.85 Squadron on 14th October. However a week later he was posted to No.310 (Czechoslovak) Squadron as a Flying Officer. On 31st August 1941 during a training flight, the cooling system of his Hurricane failed and he bailed out and suffered some injuries when he landed on the shore of Loch Oich in Scotland. His plane crashed into the loch. After recovering from his injuries he led 'B' Flight from 14th February to 15th November 1942. He achieved his first success on 4th February 1942, when, with three other pilots, he damaged a Ju88 40 miles south-west of the Scilly Isles however on 19th February he damaged his own Spitfire while landing on Perranporth airfield. On 28th April, in conjunction with Sergeant Frantisek Vindis he shot down a reconnaissance Ju88 over Bristol Bay. On 5th June he damaged a FW190 and in combat on 23rd June he shot down another FW190. During Operation *Jubilee*, on 19th August, he damaged three Do217s during his second sortie of the day. After a break from operations for two months, he returned as commanding officer in mid January 1943 and remained in command for a year. On 29th January he shot down a FW190 over the Channel, 15 miles North of Morlaix. He was awarded the Czech Military Cross, three times, the Medal for Bravery, twice, and the DFC, the latter on 8th January 1945. At the end of the war he served at the Czechoslovak Inspectorate General in London in the personnel department. After returning home he commanded the 10th Air Fighter Regiment until the Communist take-over in 1948, when he was once again forced to abandon his homeland. This time he went straight to the United Kingdom where he rejoined the RAF. Foit lived in the UK until his death on 18th June 1976.

October 1940 and served as an instructor at No.3 SFTS then retrained at No.51 OTU before to be posted to No.310 Sqn. Tour expired in November 1943 and posted to No.1 ADF. Second tour of operations in June 1944 posted from ADGB and with a short break when as an instructor with No.5 (P)AFU stayed with unit till the end of war. In July 1945, posted to Czech Depot.
P/O : 1-43, F/O : 6-44

FRÖHLICH, Bedrich   Sgt   (CZ)/RAF
3-44/8-45@   RAF No.788257
                          RAF No.195364
Posted from No.53 OTU. Czech born in Egypt. Member of Cz Army in France. Volunteered for RAF in 1942, posted to pilot course in April 1942.
F/Sgt : 8-44, P/O : 4-45

FÜRST, Bohumil   Sgt   (CZ)/RAF
8-40/3-41   RAF No.787556
Prewar CzAF fighter pilot in Air Regiment 3. Escaped to Poland in June 1939, then to France enlisting to the French Foreign Legion. Transferred to French Air Force in October 1939 then GC II/2 on Moranes. One confirmed victory with the French. Escaped to the UK arriving in July 1940 posted to No.310 Sqn the next month, serving briefly with No.605 Sqn in October 1940. Posted to No.52 OTU in March 1941. Later commisioned and served with No.24 Sqn September - December 1942 and No.510 Sqn December 1942 - August 1944. Remained in CzAF after the war, but was fired out after the Communist coup and arrested in January 1950. Realeased because of healthy reasons in August 1951. Four confirmed victories, with the French and No.310 Sqn, 1940.

GIBIAN, Tomas G.   Sgt   (CZ)/RAF
5-44/7-44   RAF No.654760
Fresh graduate posted from No.84 GSU. Czech enlisted in Canada. Posted to No.312 (Czech) Sqn until the end of war.

GÖTH, Vilem   P/O   (CZ)/RAF
7-40/10-40   RAF No.81945
Prewar CzAF fighter pilot in Air Regiment 3. Served with the FAF in 1939-1940 in Chartres (SW of Paris). Founder member of No.310 Sq in July 1940. Posted to No.501 Sqn.
†25.10.40, Hurricane I P2903, No.501 Sqn, UK.

J. HANUS

HALAMA, Stanislav   Sgt   (CZ)/RAF
10-41/4-42 (†)   RAF No.788017
Prewar CzAF fighter pilot. After retraining at No.9 SFTS was posted to No. 310 Sqn in October 1941.

HANUS, Josef   P/O   (CZ)/RAF
10-40/6-41   RAF No.82546
Posted from No.6 OTU. Prewar CzAF fighter pilot in Air Regiment 1. Escaped to France via Poland in March 1939. With FAF 1939-1940 serving with GC III/1 on Moranes. Posted to No.32 Sqn June - September 1941, No.245 Sqn September 1941 - April 1942, then night fighter pilot with No.600 Sqn, Czech flight No.68 Sqn and No.125 (Newfoundland) Sqn between April 1942 and December 1943. Returned to the UK in February 1944 with CIG until the end of the war. After the war, he returned to Czechoslovakia serving with the CzAF until the Communist coup of 1948, but emigrated to the UK soon afterwards. Served with RAF until 1968. Four confirmed destroyed with No.600 Sqn, North Africa, 1943. DFC [No.600 Sqn].
F/O : 2-41

HARTMAN, Jiri*   P/O   (CZ)/RAF
8-40/9-40, 6-42/6-43, 10-43/8-45@   RAF No.81907
Prewar CzAF fighter pilot in Air Regiment 1. Trained as fighter pilot in FAF 1939-40. He flew on Hudson to GB on 19.06.40. In August 1940 posted to No.310 Sqn, but in September 40 posted to No.12 OTU for retraining. Then served with No. 4 FPP and No.8 MU

J. HARTMAN

operations. Posted to CIG. Czechoslovak Air Attache in the USA January 1942 - September 1945. Returned to Czchecoslovakia in March 1946, but emigrated to the USA in 1948 after the Communist take over. Two confirmed victories, No.310 Sqn, Battle of Britain, 1940.

DFC : 28.10.40

HIMR, Jaroslav ✓   P/O   (CZ)/RAF
7-40/8-40   RAF No.81891
Prewar CzAF fighter pilot in Air Regiment 3. Attached to Czech Depot at Agde 1939-1940 then to GB. Posted to No.310 Sqn pending his training on Hurricane. Did not fly in operations. Posted to No.6 OTU, then No.79 Sqn September - October 1940, No.56 Sqn October 1940 - June 1941 and No.601 Sqn June - December 1941, ending his tour as flight leader. Second tour of operations as CO of No.313 (Czech) Sqn from June 1942 onwards. Two confirmed victories with No.313 Sqn, Europe, 1943. DFC [No.313 Sqn].
†24.09.43, Spitfire VB BP561, CO No.313 (Czech) Sqn, France.

till June 1941 when posted to No.55 OTU. In August 1941 posted to No.312 Sqn but without operational flying there, in October posted to No.607 Sqn and after a week to No.111 Sqn where he stayed for half a year. In June 1942 posted to No.310 Sqn as Flying Officer, becoming B flight CO on 27.02.43 succeeding F. Burda. Completed his tour in June 1943 and replaced by V. Chocholin on 01.06.43. Second tour of operations with No.310 Sqn as A Flight CO from 10.10.43 replacing H. Hrbacek. Replaced by M. Divis on 11.08.44. Last Squadron CO from 15.09.44 onwards. Transferred to the new CzAF after 1945 but left his country after the Communist coup in 1948 returning to the UK and rejoining RAF until 1957.
F/L : 2-43, S/L : 9-44

DFC : 05.11.45

HESS, Alexandr ⟋   S/L   (CZ)/RAF
7-40/2-41   RAF No.81888
WW1 veteran (infantryman). Prewar CzAF fighter pilot in Air Regiment 4. Posted as supernumerary after his training on Hurricane, being the first Czech CO of the Squadron seconding G.D.M. Blackwood. At 42, he was the oldest Czech pilot still flying in

HLAVAC, Jaroslav   Sgt   (CZ)/RAF
8-40/8-40   RAF No.787542
Prewar CzAF fighter pilot in Air Regiment 2. With FAF 1939-1940 serving with GC I/6 and GC III/7 on Moranes, then escaping to the UK. Posted to No.310 Sqn pending his training on Hurricane. Did not fly in operations. Posted to No.6 OTU, then No.79 Sqn September - October 1940, No.56 Sqn October 1940.
†10.10.40, Hurricane I P3421, No.56 Sqn, UK.

HOLECEK, Rudolf   P/O   (CZ)/RAF
7-40/9-40, 9-40/7-41   RAF No.81890
Prewar CzAF fighter pilot in Air Regiment 4. With FAF 1939-1940 serving with GC I/8 on Blochs then to GB. Founder member of No.310 Sqn in July 1940, in September posted to No.312 (Czech) Sqn just for a week, before returning to No.310 (Czech) Sqn. Tour expired in July 1941. Between July 1941 and March 1942 he served as Flying Control Officer with No.313 (Czech) Sqn. No more operational posting until the end of war, being posted to CIG from June 1942 until the end of war. Stayed with the new CzAF after 1945 but left his country after the Communist coup in 1948.
F/O : 2-41

HOLZHAUSER, Jindrich   Sgt   (CZ)/RAF
9-41/5-42   RAF No.787405
Posted from No.58 OTU. Posted to Czech Depot.

HORAK, Vaclav   W/O   (CZ)/RAF
7-43/8-43   RAF No.787561
Posted from No.313 (Czech) Sqn. Prewar CzAF fighter pilot. Served with the FAF in Toulouse 1939-1940. No.313 (Czech) Sqn August 1941 - July 1943. Posted to twin-engined training course then Czech flight No.68 Sqn February 1944 - April 1945.

HORSKY, Jindrich   Sgt   (CZ)/RAF
12-44/8-45@   RAF No.788117
Fresh graduate posted from No.57 OTU. No more details available.
F/Sgt : 3-45

HORSKY, Vladimir   Sgt   (CZ)/RAF
8-40/8-40   RAF No.787554
Prewar CzAF fighter pilot in Air Regiment 2. With

FAF 1939-1940 serving in GC I/6 on Moranes then to the UK. Posted as reserve pilot pending his training on Hurricane. Posted to No.238 Sqn.
†26.09.40, Hurricane I P3098, No.238 Sqn, UK.

HRADIL, Frantisek   P/O   (CZ)/RAF
7-40/8-40   RAF No.81899
Prewar CzAF fighter pilot in Air Regiment 2. Posted to No.310 Sqn pending his training on Hurricane. Did not fly in operations. Posted to No.6 OTU, then No.19 Sqn September 1940.
†05.11.40, Spitfire IIA P7545, No.19 Sqn, UK.

HRBACEK, Hugo***   F/L   (CZ)/RAF
5-42/10-43, 1-44/5-44   RAF No.87618
Posted from No.61 OTU. Czech born in Italy. Prewar CzAF fighter pilot in Air Regiment 4. With FAF 1939-1940 serving in GC I/7 on Moranes based in Lebannon, eventually escaping to the UK. Posted to No.1 SS in December 1940. Became A Flight CO on 01.02.43 succeeding V. Chocholin. First tour completed in October 1943, replaced by J. Hartman on

A.HESS

H.HRBACEK

S4

10.10.43 as A flight leader. Second tour of operations with No.310 Sqn from January 1944 as CO. On 21.05.44 shot down by *flak* near Lisieux (France) while attacking a train. Crash landed, evaded capture with the help of the French Resistance returning to the UK on 19.08.44. Then served at CIG. Remained with the new CzAF after 1945, became CO of No.7 Air Regiment in Brno, in 1946 CO of No.5 Air Regiment in Ceske Budejovice. He left his country shortly after the Communist coup in 1948 and rejoined the RAF.
F/L : 5-42, S/L : 1-44.

DFC : 08.01.45

HRUBY, Otakar P/O (CZ)/RAF
12-42/7-44 RAF No.117341
Posted from No.57 OTU. Prewar CzAF fighter pilot in Air Regiment 4. With FAF 1939-1940 serving with GC I/10 on Blochs then to the UK. After retraining at No.6 OTU posted to No.111 Sqn October 1940, No.313 (Czech) Sqn May 1941 - June 1942, then tour expired. Second tour with No.310 Sqn ending in July 1944.

O. HRUBY

Posted to No.17 SFTS for course on multi-engine planes and later to No.51 OTU for night fighter course. In March 1945 wounded in a crash on Mosquito. Transferred to the new CzAF after 1945 but was fired out in 1949. Arrested for two years in a working camp. Till retirement he worked as a driver and storeman. One confirmed victory with No.111 Sqn, Europe, 1940.
F/L : 4-44

DFC : 08.01.45

HUBACEK, Josef Sgt (CZ)/RAF
7-40/3-41 RAF No.787977
Prewar CzAF fighter pilot in Air Regiment 1. With FAF 1939-1940 serving in GC III/3 on Moranes. One confirmed victory with FAF 1940 before escaping to GB. Posted to No.10 MU then No.15 MU until November 1941. After a short stay in No.45 Ferry Group, posted to No.24 Sqn at the beginning 1942 until the end of the war. In 1945 he returned to his country serving as transport pilot until 1946 before becoming Chief pilot of the Czechoslovakian airlines but soon turned out in 1948. Remained in Czechoslovakia after the Communist coup. Awarded AFC on 11.11.44 [No.24 Sqn].
P/O : 2-41

HYBLER, Josef P/O (CZ)/RAF
10-40/4-42 RAF No.82551
Posted from No.6 OTU. Prewar CzAF fighter pilot in Air Regiment 4. With FAF 1939-1940 serving in GC II/2 on Moranes then to GB. Posted to No.234 Sqn April - September 1942. No more operational posting, serving until the end of the war with No.286 Sqn and No.57 OTU as instructor eventually as Flying Control Officer. After the war, he returned to his country but arrested in March 1949 and spent eleven years in prison. Emigrated to the UK in 1968.
F/O : 3-41

JANATA, Karel Sgt (CZ)/RAF
10-41/9-42 (†) RAF No.788040
Fresh graduate. Arrived to the UK through Egypt in October 1940. By mistake posted to Cz Army, transferred to RAF in February 1941. Started his training in June 1941 and posted to No.310 Sqn when the course was completed.

J. HYBLER

JANOUCH, Svatopluk P/O (CZ)/RAF
7-40/5-41 RAF No.81892

Prewar CzAF fighter pilot in Air Regiment 1. With FAF 1939-1940 serving in GC I/6 on Moranes. Three confirmed victory with FAF then to GB. Left operations in May 1941, between May and July 1941 attached to RAF Station Duxford. Since July 1941 serving as Flying Control Officer with No.312 (Czech) Sqn and in RAF Debden. In May 1942 posted to CIG and also

V. JICHA

served as Czechoslovak Liaison Officer at Nos.10 and 14 Groups of Fighter Command. From August 1944 until June 1945 Czechoslovak Air Attache in France. Remained with the new CzAF after 1945 but left the country after the Communist coup in 1948 returning to France, then in USA in 1952. One confirmed and one shared confirmed victory with the RAF, No.310 Sqn, Battle of Britain, 1940.
F/O : 2-41, F/L : 2-41

JELINEK, Egon Sgt (CZ)/RAF
6-44/3-45 RAF No.654731

Posted from No.313 (Czech) Sqn. Czech enlisted from Canada. No.313 (Czech) Sqn March - June 1944.

JELINEK, Josef Sgt (CZ)/RAF
4-45/8-45@ RAF No.788464

Fresh graduate. Posted to No.312 (Czech) Sqn as ground staff member in January 1941. Later selected for pilot course.

JICHA, Vaclav Sgt (CZ)/RAF
8-40/8-40 RAF No.787567

Prewar CzAF fighter pilot in Air Regiment 1. With FAF 1939-1940 serving in GC I/6. One confirmed and one shared confirmed victory with FAF 1940 before escaping to the UK. Posted to No.310 Sqn in August 1940, but in the same month transferred to No.6 OTU for retraining. Posted to No.1 Sqn, later No.17 Sqn November 1940 - May 1941. With No.313 (Czech) Sqn May 1941 - August 1942. No more operational posting after that date. Then test pilot at No.9 MU, since March 1943 with Vickers Armstrong Supermarine in Castle Bromwich, in May 1944 returned to No. 9 MU later transferred to No.45 MU. One confirmed victory with No.313 Sqn, Europe, 1942. DFC [No.313 Sqn] but also AFC [No.45.MU] in July 1944.
†01.02.45 as a passenger on board of Anson I NK945, No.45 MU, UK.

JILEK, Josef F/Sgt (CZ)/RAF
6-44/10-44 RAF No.787467

Posted from No.313 (Czech) Sqn. Prewar sport pilot. Attached to a group of Cz airmen in Agde 1939-1940. No.313 (Czech) Sqn May 1943 - June 1944. Tour expired in October 1944.

64

R. KANOVSKY

JIRANEK, Jarolav   F/Sgt   (CZ)/RAF
1-45/8-45@   RAF No.787321
Fresh graduate. Prewar CzAF mechanic. With Czech
Depot at Agde (France) 1939-1940 then to the UK.

JIROUDEK, Miroslav   Sgt   (CZ)/RAF
8-40/8-41   RAF No.787451
Prewar CzAF fighter pilot in Air Regiment 1. With
FAF 1939-1940 serving with GC III/1, then to the
UK. Posted to No.54 OTU for retraining as night fighter pilot. Czech flight No.68 Sqn February 1942 -
February 1943, later commissioned. Served as
transport pilot until the end of war with Nos.24 Sqn
1943-44, No.167 Sqn 1944-1945 and No.147 Sqn in
1945. Returned to Czechoslovakia after the war serving with the CSA until 1950 before to be turned out.
One shared confirmed victory with No.310 Sqn.
F/Sgt : 6-41

KAMINEK, Antonin   F/Sgt   (CZ)/RAF
5-43/9-44   RAF No.788122
Fresh graduate. Arrived to the UK from internment in
Soviet Union in June 1941. On 05.09.44 he was shot
down by flak over Netherlands. With the help of local
Underground he crossed front near Antwerp on

13.12.44 and he got back to the UK. Did not return to
operations. In 1945 he was serving with No.288 Army
Co-operation Unit.
W/O : 4-44

KANOVSKY, Rostislav   F/O   (CZ)/RAF
7-44/9-44   RAF No.131111
In 1940-1941 trained as WOP/AG, serving October
1941 - April 1942 as Air Gunner with No.311 (Czech)
Sqn (33 missions with Bomber Command, 8 more
with Coastal Command). Selected for a pilot course,
then No.310 Sqn in July 1944. Made PoW on
05.09.44, liberated 02.05.45.

KAUCKY, Jan   Sgt   (CZ)/RAF
7-40/3-41   RAF No.787976
Prewar CzAF pilot. With FAF 1939-1940 attached to a
group of Cz airmen in Agde 1939-1940. Posted to
No.52 OTU. Instructor pilot then test pilot 1941 - 1943
before becoming transport pilot with No.511 Sqn between March 1944 and end of war. After his return to
Czechoslovakia served with the Czechoslovak Airlines
and later as test pilot of Ministry of Transport till
September 1950 when reached the UK aboard a Dakota
together with E. Prchal and J. Rechka.

J. KAUER

69

B. KIMLICKA

Commander between 15.02.41 succeeding F. Weber. Replaced by C.A.W. Bodie on 08.03.41. Posted to No.485 (N.Z.) Sqn as CO. Five sorties with the Czechs. One confirmed victory with No.485 Sqn. DFC [No.485 Sqn].
F/L : 2-41

KOMINEK, Josef   Sgt   (CZ)/RAF
7-40/6-41 (†)   RAF No.787980
Prewar CzAF fighter pilot in Air Regiment 2. With Polish Air Force in 1939. Escaped to France via Poland and Romania in 1939, no record about service with FAF. Became founder member of No.310 Sqn in July 1940. Two confirmed victories with No.310 Sqn, Battle of Britain, 1940.

KOPECKY, Miroslav   Sgt   (CZ)/RAF
7-40/8-40   RAF No.787984
Prewar CzAF fighter pilot in Air Regiment 1. With FAF 1939-1940 serving in DAT Tours. Reserve pilot in No.310 Sqn pending his training on Hurricanes. Later posted to No.111 Sqn for one month, then to No.253 Sqn September 1940 - March 1941. No more operational posting until the end of war, being flying instructor most of the time. After 1948, he settled in Rhodesia.

KAUER, Jaroslav   Sgt   (CZ)/RAF
9-44/12-44 (†)   RAF No.787634
Posted from No.313 (Czech) Sqn. Prewar CzAF mechanic. With Czech Depot at Agde (France) 1939-1940. Between September 1940 - April 1942 armourer with No.312 (Czech) Sqn. Selected for a pilot course, after after graduation posted to No.313 (Czech) Sqn in July 1944.

KIMLICKA, Bohuslav*   P/O   (CZ)/RAF
8-40/9-42, 6-43/11-43, 1-44/1-44   RAF No. 82553
Prewar CzAF fighter pilot in Air Regiment 6. With FAF 1939-1940 serving with ELD Chartres, GC II/10 on Blochs and GC I/6 on Moranes then to GB. Posted to No.310 Sqn from August 1940, but in September 1940 went for a week to No.312 (Czech) Sqn. Posted to No.313 (Czech) Sqn in September 1942 where became B flight leader. Second tour in June 1943 with No.310 Sqn becoming B Flight leader on 24.09.43 succeeding V. Chocholin. Replaced by V. Raba on 06.12.43 for a rest. Returned to No.310 Sqn in January 1944 and he finished second tour the same month. Rest of war spent at CIG. In 1948 emigrated to the UK.
F/L : 9-40

KNIGHT, Martin W. B. *   F/O   (NZ)/RAF
2-41/3-41   RAF No.37408
Posted from No.257 (Burma) Squadron. B Flight

M.W.B. KNIGHT

74

1940 and No.17 Sqn between September 1940 and June 1941 before going for rest. Then CO of Czechoslovak Depot, later served as staff officer at CIG until the end of war. Returned to Czechoslovakia in 1945 but emigrated to the UK in 1948.

Kosina, Karel   Sgt   (cz)/RAF
8-40/12-40, 3-42/4-42, 12-42/5-44, 11-44/5-45
                                        RAF No.787539
                                        RAF No.112734
Prewar CzAF member. FAF 1939-1940 serving with GC III/7 and I/6 on Moranes then to GB. Posted to No.310 Sqn in August 1940, in September 1940 moved for a week to No.312 (Czech) Sqn, then returned back to No.310 Sqn. Posted to No.19 Sqn in December 1940 - August 1941. Second tour of operations in March 1942 again at No.310 Sqn but as Pilot Officer and stayed there till end of war. Re-posted to No.310 Sqn for a third time from No.84 GSU. In May 1945, posted to GCS.
F/O : 3-43, F/L : 4-44

Kopriva, Josef   Sgt   (cz)/RAF
8-40/12-40   RAF No.787582
Prewar CzAF fighter pilot and FAF 1939-1940 serving with GC II/2 on Moranes then to the UK. Posted to No.310 Sqn in August 1940 and to No.19 Sqn between December 1940 - June 1941. No.255 Sqn June - September 1941, then Czech Flight No.68 Sqn until June 1942. CIG until the end of war. Returned to Czechoslovakia but emigrated to the UK in 1948.

Körber, Karel   W/O   (cz)/RAF
8-42/5-43 (†)   RAF No.787699
Posted from No.21 GRS. Czech born in Hungary. Prewar CzAF fighter pilot. With FAF serving with GC II/3 on Moranes and Dewoitines. Two shared confirmed victories in France 1940 before escaping to GB. First tour of operations with No.32 Sqn in October 1940 - October 1941 and with No.222 (Natal) Sqn October - December 1941. Then served as an instructor, for second tour posted to No.310 Sqn in August 1942.

Kordula, Frantisek   P/O   (cz)/RAF
7-40/8-40   RAF No.82156
Prewar CzAF fighter pilot in Air Regiment 4. Served with FAF 1939-40 as staff officer in Paris. Posted to No.310 Sqn as reserve pilot and then posted to No.6 OTU for retraining. Posted to No.1 Sqn in September

Koukal, Josef   Sgt   (cz)/RAF
7-40/9-40   RAF No.787979
Prewar CzAF fighter pilot in Air Regiment 1. Joined Polish air force in 1939. With FAF serving in Tours 1939-1940 then to the UK. Founder member of No.310 Sqn in July 1940. Badly wounded in action on 07.09.40. Later commissioned and returned to flying

J . KUCERA

KREDBA, Miroslav*   P/O   (CZ)/RAF
7-40/2-42 (†)   RAF No.81895
Prewar CzAF fighter pilot in Air Regiment 4. With Czech Depot at Agde 1939-1940 then to GB. Replaced C.A.W. Bodie as B Flight Commander on 03.06.41 until his death. Replaced by E. Foit.
F/O : 2-41, F/L : 6-41

KUBAK, Josef   Sgt   (CZ)/RAF
7-40/3-41   RAF No.787983
Prewar CzAF bomber pilot. With FAF serving in Pau, Châteauroux and Blida (North Africa) 1939-1940 before escaping to the UK. Founder member of No.310 Sqn in July 1940, moved to No.312 (Czech) Sqn in September 1940 and after week returned back to No.310 Sqn. Posted to No.19 Sqn in March 1941 for a week, then to No.118 Sqn for two weeks and eventually to No.32 Sqn in April. Tour completed in May 1941 and for the rest of war he served as an instructor in England and Canada.

KUCERA, Jiri V.   Sgt   (CZ)/RAF
8-40/8-40   RAF No.787658
Prewar CzAF fighter pilot in Air Regiment 4. With FAF 1939-1940 serving in GC I/6 on Moranes then went to GB. Posted to No.310 Sqn in August 1940 but after few days posted to No.6 OTU for retraining on Hurricanes. Then posted to No.238 Sqn in September. Badly injured in accident in November 1940, returning to operations in May 1941 with No.501 Sqn before to be posted to the newly created No.313 (Czech) Sqn where he completed his tour in June 1943. Then passed courses at SFTS College, Nos.9 and 8 OTUs, ending the war with No.544 Sqn (Photo Reconnaissance) from August 1944. Stayed with the new CzAF after 1945 but fired out in 1949. Then he worked as a worker in Skoda factory in Plzen. Two confirmed victories with No.238 Sqn, Battle of Britain, 1940.

unit in January 1943 (after 22 plastic surgeries) with No.5 (P)AFU and No.53 OTU and then for as second tour of operations with No.312 (Czech) Sqn May - August 1943. With CIG from November 1943 until the end of war. Returned to Czechoslovakia in 1945 being test pilot but after short time was discarded as invalid. Living in very poor condition on small invalid rent, he avoided Communist persecution.

KRATOCHVIL, Miroslav   Sgt   (CZ)/RAF
1-45/5-45   RAF No.788479
Posted from No.57 OTU. Czech born in Russia. Volunteered for RAF service in 1942 as member of No.11 Cz Infantry Battalion in the Middle East. After finishing pilot training posted to No.310 Sqn in January 1945 and stayed with unit till end of war. Later moved to the UK.
F/Sgt : 4-45

KRAVEC, Johan   F/Sgt   (CZ)/RAF
6-44/8-45@   RAF No.654759
Slovak enlisted in Canada. After finishing pilot training posted to No.310 Sqn in June 1944 and stayed with unit till end of war.
W/O : 5-45

LAMBERTON, Karel   Sgt   (CZ)/RAF
7-44/10-44   RAF No.788101
Fresh graduate. In July 1941 posted to No.312 (Czech) Sqn as ground staff member, later selected for a pilot course. Posted to No.312 (Czech) Sqn in October 1944 and stayed with this unit till the end of war.

J. MACHACEK

K. MACURA

85

LANDSMAN, Jindrich   F/Sgt   (CZ)/RAF
10-44/6-45 (†)   RAF No.788129
Posted from No.61 OTU. Czech born in Slovakia. Arrived to the UK from internment in Soviet Union in June 1941 and in February 1942 posted to pilot course. No.310 Sqn in October 1944.
W/O : 4-45

LATIMER, Jerrard***   F/L   RAF
7-40/7-41   RAF No.39286
Prewar RAF pilot with a SSC at that time under the name of Jefferies (later changed to Latimer in March 1941). Served with No.17 Sqn September 1939 - May 1940 and No.85 Sqn June - July 1940 before to be posted to No.310 Sqn as first B Flight from 12.07.40 before succeeding to G. Blackwood at the head of the unit. Replaced as B Flight Commander by F. Weber on 01.01.41. Posted as to No.1455 Night Fighter Flight (Turbinlite) as CO July 1941 - January 1942. Killed during a raid to Stuttgard as extra aircrew. Five confirmed victories and three shared confirmed victories with Nos.17 and 310 Sqns, France and Battle of Britain.
S/L : 1-41
†15.04.43, Lancaster III ED752, No.106 Sqn, France.

DFC : LG 01.10.40

LYSICKY, Vojtech   Sgt   (CZ)/RAF
5-42/5-43, 10-43/4-44 (†)   RAF No.787570
Prewar CzAF fighter pilot in Air Regiment 3. FAF 1939-1940 serving in Toulouse before reaching GB. After retraining posted to No.19 Sqn in July 1941 and posted to No.310 Sqn in May 1942 where finished first tour in May 1943, posted to No.3 ADF. Started second tour again with No.310 Sqn in October 1943.
F/Sgt : 10-42

MACHACEK, Jiri   P/O   (CZ)/RAF
8-40/9-40   RAF No.82560
Prewar CzAF fighter pilot in Air Regiment 4. With Czech Depot at Agde in France 1939-1940, then GB. Posted to No.310 Sqn as reserve pilot pending his Hurricane training in August 1940, in the same month transferred to No.6 OTU for retraining. Posted to No.145 Sqn in September 1940.
†08.07.41, Spitfire VA R7218, No.145 Sqn, Belgium.

MACURA, Karel   Sgt   (CZ)/RAF
12-44/2-45 (†)   RAF No.788497
Posted from No.57 OTU. Volunteered for RAF service in 1942 as member of No.11 Cz Infantry Battalion in the Middle East. After finishing pilot training posted to No.310 Sqn in December 1944.

MALY, Jaroslav P/O (CZ)/RAF
7-40/12-40 RAF No.81909

Prewar CzAF member. Between 1936 and 1939 Czechoslovak military and air Attaché in Germany. With FAF 1939-1940 serving in EC Chartres and as a staff officer in Paris before escaping to the UK. Seconded G.L. Sinclair as Flight Leader. Posted to CIG in London as staff officer.
F/L : 9-40
†06.06.41 of natural cause.

MANAK, Jiri P/O (CZ)/RAF
8-40/9-40 RAF No.81896

Prewar CzAF observer in Air Regiment 6. With FAF in 1939-1940 completing fighter training but did not reach operational unit. Escaped to the UK. Posted as reserve pilot to No.310 Sqn pending his training on Hurricane, but in September posted to No.6 OTU, then No.601 Sqn November 1940 - November 1941, and eventually served instructor with No.61 OTU. Second tour of operations with No.81 Sqn July - August 1942, No.611 Sqn August - September 1942. In September 1942 posted No.182 Sqn on Typhoons, becoming A Flight leader in October. In May 1943, posted to No.198 Sqn as CO. Shot down and made PoW on 28.08.43, being liberated

on 02.05.45. In August 1945 posted to No.312 (Czech) Sqn for return to Czechoslovakia remaining with the new CzAF after 1945 till 1948 as test pilot. Since 1948 he worked as test pilot at Ministry of Transport, arrested in 1950, released in 1951, later reinstated by the authorities. Two confirmed victories with No.601 Sqn, Europe, 1941. DFC [No.198 Sqn].

MAREK, Frantisek Sgt (CZ)/RAF
7-40/8-40 RAF No.787975

Prewar CzAF fighter pilot in Air Regiment 1. With FAF serving in Avord 1939-40 then to GB. Founder member of No.310 Sqn but posted to No.19 Sqn in August 1940.
†14.09.40, Spitfire I R6625, No.19 Sqn, UK.

MARES, Frantisek W/O (CZ)/RAF
7-44/12-44 RAF No.787653
  RAF No.185291

Prewar CzAF member under training as fighter pilot. With FAF 1939-1940 and completed his training but did not reach operational unit then reached GB. Posted first to No.601 Sqn November 1940 - March 1942, No.610 Sqn March - May 1942, No.313

J . MANAK

A . MEIER

(Czech) Sqn May - June 1942 then No.312 (Czech) Sqn June - September 1942. Second tour of operations with No.313 (Czech) Sqn March 1943 - June 1943 but withdrawn from operations for medical reasons. Posted to No.310 Sqn from No.53 OTU but continued to have medical problems and had to leave regulary for hospitalisation his unit until the end of war. Settled in England after the war. One confirmed and three shared confirmed victories with Nos.310 and 313 Sqns, Europe, 1941-1942. DFM [No.312 Sqn].
P/O : 9-44

MASEK, Stanislav   P/O   (CZ)/RAF
7-43/11-44   RAF No.133435
Fresh graduate. Czech born in GB. May have been found unfit for flying and in November 1944 posted to No.84 GSU. Later Czechoslovak Depot where he died.
†22.07.45 of natural cause.

MEIER, Augustin   Sgt   (CZ)/RAF
2-43/5-44 (†)   RAF No.788332
Posted from No.312 (Czech) Sqn. No.312 Sqn in February 1943 for a week only before to be posted to No.310 Sqn.
F/Sgt : 11-43

K. MRAZEK

MLEJNECKY, Frantisek   Sgt   (CZ)/RAF
10-40/5-41, 6-41/1-43   RAF No.787503
With FAF 1939-1940 serving in ELD Chartres, GC I/6 on Moranes then escaped to the UK. After retraining posted to No.85 Sqn in October 1940, moved to No.310 Sqn in the same month. In May 1941 posted to No. 257 (Burma) Sqn but returned the following month to No.310 Sqn to complete his first tour in January 1943. Started a second tour in July 1943 with No.313 Sqn, but posted to No.312 Sqn in August 1943 and finished second tour in October 1944.
F/Sgt : 8-41

MORAVEC, Miroslav   F/Sgt   (CZ)/RAF
10-43/6-44 (†)   RAF No.787609
Prewar pilot. With Czech Depot at Agde 1939-1940 then went to GB. Sent to a pilot course in February 1942. After finishing pilot training posted to No. 310 Sqn in October 1943. All his family was executed in 1942 by the Nazis following R. Heydrich assassination.

MORCH, Josef   Sgt   (CZ)/RAF
10-43/7-44   RAF No.788134
Posted from No.61 OTU. Arrived to the UK from internment in Soviet Union in June 1941, in February 1942 posted to pilot course. Tour expired July 1944, then till December 1944 in Czechoslovak Depot. Then January and February 1945 passed Airfield Controller Course.

MRAZEK, Karel   P/O   (CZ)/RAF
8-40/8-40   RAF No.82561
Prewar CzAF fighter pilot in Air Regiment 2. Served with the FAF 1939-1940 in a towing-target unit GR 4/108 then reached GB. Posted to No.310 Sqn in August 1940, but sent to No.6 OTU for retraining. Battle of Britain veteran with Nos.43 and 46 Sqns serving with the latter between September 1940 - April 1941. Then served briefly with No.257 (Burma) Sqn before being posted in May to No.313 (Czech) Sqn as Flight Commander before taking command of the unit in December 1941. CO Exeter Wing June 1942 - April 1943. No more operational posting until the end of war, the last posting being liaison officer between Fighter Command and Czechoslovak Fighter Wing from March 1945. Returned to Czechoslavakia in 1945. Arrested by the Communists in 1948 and removed from service. Three confirmed and one shared victories with Nos.46, 313 Sqns, and Exeter wing

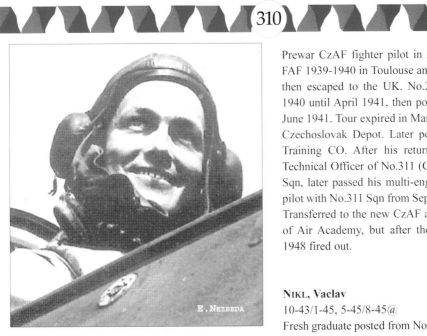

E. NEZBEDA

1940 - 1942. DSO [Exeter wing], DFC [No.313 Sqn].

NAGY, Michael S. F/Sgt (CZ)/RAF
9-44/8-45@ RAF No.654738
RAF No.187263

Posted from No.313 (Czech) Sqn. Slovak born in Indiana, USA. After his pilot training completed posted to No.313 Sqn in May 1944 - September 1944.
P/O : 12-44, F/O : 5-45

NAVRATIL, Antonin P/O (CZ)/RAF
7-40/8-40 RAF No.81897

Prewar CzAF fighter pilot in Air Regiment 3. With FAF 1939-1940 serving GC I/8 on Blochs then to GB. Founder member of No.310 Sqn in July 1940. Posted to No.312 Sqn August 1940 - March 1941. Then various staff functions at Czechoslovak Inspectorate General (CIG) till October 1944 when he moved to Soviet Union where he finished the war as a chief staff officer of the 1st Cz Air Division.

NEDELKA, Vladimir Sgt (CZ)/RAF
12-44/8-45@ RAF No.788389

Posted from No.57 OTU. Joined Czech forces from Argentina.
F/Sgt : 4-45

NEZBEDA, Egon F/O (CZ)/RAF
6-41/3-42 RAF No.82565

Posted from No.501 Sqn. Czech born in Germany.

Prewar CzAF fighter pilot in Air Regiment 2. With FAF 1939-1940 in Toulouse and Blida (North Africa) then escaped to the UK. No.24 Sqn from Summer 1940 until April 1941, then posted to No.501 Sqn in June 1941. Tour expired in March 1942 and posted to Czechoslovak Depot. Later posted to Canada to as Training CO. After his return to the UK became Technical Officer of No.311 (Czechoslovak) Bomber Sqn, later passed his multi-engined rating. Liberator pilot with No.311 Sqn from September 1944 onwards. Transferred to the new CzAF after 1945 as professor of Air Academy, but after the Communist coup in 1948 fired out.

NIKL, Vaclav Sgt (CZ)/RAF
10-43/1-45, 5-45/8-45@ RAF No.788136

Fresh graduate posted from No.84 GSU. Prewar pilot. With PAF in 1939. In February 1942 posted to pilot course. Wounded on 05.01.45 when his aircraft was hit and destroyed on ground by a Boeing B-17. Returned to the unit in May 1945.
W/O : 5-45

PAVLU, Otto P/O (CZ)/RAF
2-43/4-43 (†) RAF No.117614

Posted from No.65 Sqn. Prewar CzAF fighter pilot. With FAF 1939-1940 serving in GC II/3 on Dewoitines, then to GB. No.1 Sqn October 1940 - August 1941, No.54 Sqn August - November 1941, No.222 (Natal) Sqn November 1941 - January 1942. No.65 Sqn January 1942 - February 1943.
F/O : 3-43

PERINA, Karel W/O (CZ)/RAF
2-45/8-45@ RAF No.788140

Posted from No.312 (Czech) Sqn. Arrived to the UK from internment in Soviet Union in June 1941. In February 1942 posted to a pilot course. No.313 (Czech) Sqn October 1943 - May 1944, No.312 (Czech) from May 1944 until posted to No.310 Sqn.

PERNICA, Karel Sgt (CZ)/RAF
12-41/7-43, 2-45/8-45@ RAF No.787387
RAF No.185293

Fresh graduate. With FAF 1939-1940 as pilot under training in Pau, Chartres and Cazaux. Started pilot course in August 1941 completed in December. First tour expired in July 1943. Second tour of operations

M. PETR

in February 1944 with No.312 (Czech) Sqn before to be posted to No.310 Sqn in February 1945 as Pilot Officer.
F/Sgt : 10-42, F/O : 4-45

PEROUTKA, Stanislav F/O (CZ)/RAF
2-43/2-45 RAF No.117372
Czech born in Carpathian Russia. Prewar CzAF fighter pilot in Air Regiment 4. With French Air Force 1939, serving with GC II/3 on Moranes and Dewoitines. Claimed one confirmed victory with FAF before escaping to the UK. No.312 (Czech) Sqn September 1940 - October 1942, then tour expired. Second tour of operations with No.310 (Czech) Sqn starting in February 1943. Posted to Czechoslovak Depot.

PETR, Miroslav Sgt (CZ)/RAF
7-41/1-43 (†) RAF No.787602
Posted from No.52 OTU. Prewar CzAF fighter pilot. With Cz airmen at Agde 1939-1940 then to GB. After retraining, No.24 Sqn, No.1 SofAC and No.52 OTU.
F/Sgt : 4-42, W/O : 10-42

PIPA, Josef F/O (CZ)/RAF
7-44/7-44 RAF No.145101
Posted from No.313 (Czech) Sqn. Prewar CzAF fighter pilot in Air Regiment 2. With FAF 1939-1940 serving with GC I/1 on Blochs before reaching GB. One tour of operations with No.43 Sqn October 1940 - April 1942, No.81 Sqn in May 1942, then to newly created No.313 (Czech) Sqn May - June 1942 and No.312 (Czech) Sqn until June - November 1942 when his tour expired. Second tour from February 1943 with No.313 Sqn, moved to No.310 Sqn in July 1944 for a week only, achieving six sorties with No.310 Sqn. Posted to No.312 (Czech) Sqn ending the war as B flight CO. One confirmed V-1 with No.310 Sqn, Europe 1944.

PLZAK, Stanislav Sgt (CZ)/RAF
8-40/8-40 RAF No.787502
Prewar CzAF fighter pilot in Air Regiment 1. With FAF in 1939-1940 serving with GC II/2 on Moranes. Three shared confirmed victories with FAF then to GB. Posted as reserve pilot pending his training. Posted to No.19 Sqn until his death.
†07.08.41, Spitfire IIA P7771, No.19 Sqn, France.

POPELKA, Viktor Sgt (CZ)/RAF
12-41/6-43, 2-45/8-45@ RAF No.787587
  RAF No.178523
Fresh graduate. Prewar pilot under training. Serving with FAF 1939-40 in Istres and La Rochelle before escaping to the UK. Started pilot course in August 1941, then posted to No.310 Sqn. Posted to No.1 ADF when tour expired. Second tour with No.312 (Czech) Sqn February 1944 - February 1945. Commissioned, then posted to No.310 Sqn as Flying Officer and stayed there till end of war. DFC [No. 312 Sqn].
F/Sgt : 10-42

POSLUZNY, Ondrej P/O (CZ)/RAF
8-40/9-40, 9-40/3-41 RAF No.82568
Prewar CzAF member. With FAF serving with GC III/4 in Morocco (North Africa) before reaching GB. Briefly posted to No.310 Sqn in Ausgust 1940, then shortly to No.312 (Czech) Sqn in September 1940 before to be posted back to No.310 Sqn in the same month. In March 1941 briefly posted to Nos.19 and 118 Sqns and then No.32 Sqn in April 1942 becoming A Flight Leader.
†26.06.42, Hurricane IIB Z3088, No.32 Sqn, France.

POSTOLKA, Jindrich Sgt (CZ)/RAF
8-40/8-40 RAF No.787456

Czech born in Austria. Prewar CzAF fighter pilot in Air Regiment 1. With FAF 1939-1940 serving in GC I/1 on Blochs, then to GB. One confirmed victory with FAF. Posted to Czechoslovak Depot and sent for retraining to No.56 OTU in February 1941. No further information about any operational duty. Between February 1942 and August 1943 served as Link Trainer Instructor with No.1429 Czech Operational Training Flight and No.6 (C) OTU, later till the end of war in the same post at No.311 (Czechoslovak) Sqn.

PRCHAL, Eduard M. Sgt (CZ)/RAF
7-40/3-41 RAF No.787982

Prewar CzAF fighter pilot in Air Regiment 5. With FAF 1939-1940, serving with GC I/8 on Blochs. Three confirmed victories with FAF before escaping to the UK. Founder member of No.310 Sqn in July 1940. Posted to No.55 OTU as flying instructor, then transferred for night fighter course to No.54 OTU.

No.255 Sqn August - September 1941, then Czech flight No.68 Sqn September 1941 - April 1942. Between April and June 1942 with No.116 Sqn and No.24 Sqn June - December 1942. In December 1942 posted to No.511 Sqn. On 04.07.44 he was piloting Liberator II AL523 which crashed into the sea after take off from Gibraltar killing sixteen people aboard including Polish General W. Sikorski. Prchal was the only survivor. Two confirmed and one shared confirmed victories, No.310 Sqn, Battle of Britain, 1940. After the war served with the new CzAF, in 1946 moved to Czechoslovak Airlines before reaching GB in September 1950 aboard Dakota together with J. Kaucky and J. Rechka. In 1952 moved to the USA. *F/Sgt : 3-41*

PROKOPEC, Josef Sgt (CZ)/RAF
1-44/10-44 RAF No.78843

Fresh graduate. Arrived to the UK from internment in Soviet Union in June 1941, in February 1942 posted to pilot course. Posted to No.312 (Czech) October 1944 - August 1945.

E. PRCHAL

R. PUDA

Supermarine Spitfire F.IXC BS126, No.310 (Czechoslovak) Squadron, Flight Sergeant J. Prokopec, North Weald, UK, September 1944. This aircraft is carrying a 90 gallons slipper tank.

Few photographs taken for the propaganda or on the field.
Top, taken at Martlesham Heath in July 1941,
from left to right :
Sgt Jindrich Skirka, F/L Patrick P.G. Davies, F/O Bohuslav
Kimlicka, S/L Frantisek Weber, unknown Intelligence officer,
F/O Egon Nezbeda, F/Sgt Miroslav Jiroudek.
(IWM HU40538)

Left, taken at Duxford beginning 1941,
from left to right :
F/O Stanislav Zimprich, unknown, Sgt Alois Dvorak (standing
on the wing), F/Lt Frantisek Dolezal, F/O Vladimir Zaoral and
F/O Josef Hanus. (J. Rajlich)

Bottom, taken at Perranporth during Spring 1942,
from left to right :
F/L Vaclav Sikl, F/L Vladislav Chocholin, unknown, F/Sgt
Frantisek Vindis, W/O Jindrich Skirka, W/O Karel Korber, unk-
nown, F/Sgt Antonin Skach (behind Korber´s cap) and F/Sgt
Miloslav Petr. (J. Rajlich)

J. RECHKA

PUDA, Rajmund   Sgt   (CZ)/RAF
8-40/1-41   RAF No.787623
Prewar CzAF fighter pilot in Air Regiment 1. With FAF 1939-1940 serving in GC II/4 on Curtisses. Three shared confirmed victories with FAF then to GB. Posted to No.310 Sqn in August 1940. Posted to No.610 Sqn. Then served as an instructor between March 1941 and October 1943. Posted to No.24 Sqn October 1943 - August 1944, Metropolitan Communication Sqn (MCS) until July 1945. Two confirmed shared victories, No.310 Sqn, Battle of Britain, 1940. After the war served with the new CzAF, in 1946 moved to Czechoslovak Airlines. In April 1948 he was sent to first conference of transport pilots in London and decided to stay in UK. Rejoined the RAF and served until 1954.

RABA, Vaclav*   F/L   (CZ)/RAF
4-43/9-44   RAF No.82569
Posted from No.57 OTU. Prewar CzAF fighter pilot in Air Regiment 5. With FAF 1939-1940 serving in Toulouse then escaped to the UK. No.247 (China-British) Sqn April 1941, then No.501 Sqn April 1941 - May 1942, No.313 (Czech) Sqn May - October 1942 ending his first tour at that time. Second tour of operations with No.310 Sqn. On 06.12.1943 he was appointed B flight commander succeeding B. Kimlicka, replaced on 22.05.44 by F. Bernard, to take command the Squadron. Posted to CIG as a staff officer until the end of war. Remained with the new CzAF after 1945 but left his country before the Communist coup in 1948 returning to the UK.
S/L : 5-44

RADIC, Antonin   Sgt   (CZ)/RAF
7-44/8-45@   RAF No.788272
Fresh graduate. Slovak. No more details available.
F/Sgt : 3-45

RECHKA, Josef   Sgt   (CZ)/RAF
8-40/6-41   RAF No.787507
Prewar CzAF fighter pilot in Air Regiment 1. With FAF 1939-1940 serving in GC III/7 and I/6 on Moranes then to GB. Posted to HQ FPP, then to No.27 MU in October 1941 before serving with Ferry Command in November that year. In December 1942 posted to No.24 Sqn, No.512 Sqn August 1943 - February 1944, then returning to No.24 Sqn. Ended the war with No.147 Sqn from April 1945. Commissionned during the war. One shared confirmed victory, No.310 Sqn, Battle of Britain, 1940. After the war served with the new CzAF, later moved to Czechoslovak Airlines before reaching GB in September 1950 aboard Dakota together with J. Kaucky and E. Prchal. AFC [No. 24 Sqn].
F/Sgt : 6-41

REHOR, Frantisek   Sgt   (CZ)/RAF
6-44/8-44 (†)   RAF No.787229
Posted from No.84 GSU. No details available except that he was at Agde in France in 1939 - 1940 (Czech Depot).

V.RIDKOSIL

RIDKOSIL, Vaclav   F/L   (CZ)/RAF
9-42/2-43 (†)   RAF No.82944
Posted from No.58 OTU. Prewar CzAF fighter pilot in Air Regiment 6. Served with FAF 1939-1940 as staff officer in Paris before escaping to the UK. Served as Intelligence Officer with No.310 Sqn from June 1940 and May 1941 then sent to No.2 SS, before returning to No.310 Sqn as Intelligence Officer. In February 1942, posted to No.312 (Czech) Sqn as Intelligence Officer before to be sent to a pilot course.

ROHACEK, Rudolf   P/O   (CZ)/RAF
7-40/8-40   RAF No.81910
Prewar CzAF fighter pilot in Air Regiment 4. With FAF 1939-1940 serving in Chartres. Posted to No.6 OTU for retraining in August 1940. Posted to No.601 Sqn in September 1940, then to No.238 Sqn October 1940 - April 1941, No.312 (Czech) Sqn April 1941 - April 1942.
†27.04.42, Spitfire VB AD553, No.312 (Czech) Sqn, UK.

RYPL, Frantisek   F/L   (cz)/RAF
7-40/12-40   RAF No.81900
Prewar CzAF fighter pilot in Air Regiment 3. With FAF 1939-1940 serving in Bordeaux, then to GB. Became founder member of No.310 Sqn in July 1940, seconding J. Jefferies as of B Flight. In December moved to Czechoslovak Inspectorate General in London as staff officer. In Summer 1942 passed night fighter course and in September 1942 posted to No.307 (Polish) Night Fighter Sqn. Withdrawn from operational duty in November 1942 following a flying accident on Beaufighter. In August 1944 he left the RAF and moved to Soviet Union where he became leading navigator of 1st Cz Air Division in January 1945. On 09.05.45 he became the first Czechoslovak airmen who landed in Prague in a crew of Petljakov Pe-2. He was one of the few RAF airmen who decided to collaborate with Communist regime and after the Communist coup in 1948 being promoted to the rank of Major General the same year and stayed in this rank till retirement.

SALA, Jaroslav   F/Sgt   (CZ)/RAF
8-41/1-43 (†)   RAF No.787450
Posted from No.55 OTU. Prewar CzAF fighter pilot with Air Regiment 2. With FAF 1939-1940 serving at Avord, Istres and Châteauroux then to GB. After

K. SEDA

retraining with No.24 Sqn and No. 1 SS by January 1941, then No.55 OTU.
W/O : 10-42

SEDA, Karel   Sgt   (CZ)/RAF
8-40/4-41   RAF No.787549
Prewar CzAF fighter pilot with Air Regiment 3 and pilot of Czechoslovak Airlines. With FAF 1939-1940 serving in GC II/2 on Moranes then escaped to the UK. One tour of operations with No.310 Sqn, but withdrawn from operations due of his age, 32 in April 1941. Flew with various Maintenance Units in the next two years. In May 1943 posted to No.54 OTU, and in July 1943 posted to Czech Flight No.68 Night Fighter Sqn. In January 1945 posted to No.105 (T) OTU and then posted to Metropolitan Communications Sqn (MCS). Commissioned during the war. One confirmed victory, No.68 Sqn, Europe, 1944. Remained with the new CzAF after 1945 for a short time, then Captain of Czechoslovak Airlines in 1946, in 1949 fired out and in the same year arrested for fourteen years while caught in trying to escape with the help of communist agent. After release in 1958, he worked as electrician.

SIKA, Jaroslav   Sgt   (CZ)/RAF
3-42/7-42, 3-43/7-44   RAF No.787382
                  RAF No.158967
Posted from No.57 OTU. Prewar CzAF fighter pilot. With FAF 1939-1940 serving in GC I/8. Three shared

V. SIKL

HQ No.12 Group. Later first CO of No.313 (Czech) Sqn May - September 1941, then CO No.79 Sqn September - December 1941. Another tour of operations in March 1943 with various units awaiting reappointment, then CO of No.56 Sqn September 1943 - May 1944. No more operational posting after that date. Ten confirmed victories with Nos.19 and 310 Sqns, Europe 1940. DFC [No.19 Sqn].

SKACH, Antonin   Sgt   (CZ)/RAF
9-41/6-43, 7-44/9-44 (†)   RAF No.788032
Posted from No.1 Sqn. Prewar CzAF fighter pilot. Arrived to the UK from internment in Soviet Union in October 1940. For short time posted to No.2 SS, in May 1941 started retraining, then posted to No.1 Sqn in July 1941 before joining No.310 Sqn. Tour expired in June 1943 and posted to No.3 ADF. Second tour of operations with No.312 (Czech) Sqn February - July 1944, before to be posted to No.310 Sqn for the second time as Warrant Officer.

SKARVADA, Zdenek   Sgt   (CZ)/RAF
7-41/2-42   RAF No.788031
Posted from No.52 OTU. Prewar CzAF fighter pilot in Air Regiment 4. He joined Polish Air Force and served as instructor and with *Eskadra Cwiczebna Obsewatorow* in SPL Deblin. After the invasion of Poland he escaped to Soviet Union but was interned during a couple of months, arriving to the UK in October 1940. Quick re-training with No.52 OTU in June 1941 before posted to No.310 Sqn. Made PoW in February 1942. He was liberated on 02.05.45.

SKIRKA, Jindrich   Sgt   (CZ)/RAF
11-40/4-43, 6-43/11-44   RAF No.787654
          RAF No.145003
Posted from No.52 OTU. Prewar CzAF fighter pilot in Air Regiment 2. With Czech Depot at Agde 1939-40, then to the UK. After retraining posted to No.310 Sqn in November 1940. Short rest in Spring 1943 but served until November 1944 returning commissioned. Posted out for training as Operation Room controller.
W/O : 4-42, P/O : 6-43, F/O : 10-43

SKREKA-BAUDOIN, Vojtech   Sgt   (CZ)/RAF
7-44/8-45@   RAF No.788295
Came from No.11 Cz Infantry Batallion from the Middle East. After finishing pilot training posted to

confirmed victories with FAF. Then to GB. After retraining at No.6 OTU posted to No.43 Sqn October 1940 - May 1941, No.313 (Czech) Sqn May - July 1941, No.452 (RAAF) Sqn for two days and then to No.72 Sqn for few days where finished first tour. For old injury suffered in France withdrawn from operations and from August 1941 posted as an instructor to No.57 OTU. Returned to operations with No.310 Sqn but in June 1942 posted to No.2 DF. Returned to No.310 Sqn in March 1943 posted from No.11 (P)AFU and completing his second tour in July 1944. To No.51 OTU, night fighting training unit, then No.25 Sqn from April 1945 till end of war. One confirmed victory, No.72 Sqn, Europe, 1941. After the war served with the new CzAF, but was had to leave it for medical reasons.
P/O : 11-43, F/O : 3-44

SIKL, Vaclav   F/O   (CZ)/RAF
6-41/2-42   RAF No.82218
Prewar CzAF fighter pilot in Air Regiment 5. With FAF 1939-1940 serving in GC II/2 on Moranes then went to GB. Then Operation Room CIG. No further details.

SINCLAIR, Gordon L. *   F/L   RAF
7-40/12-40   RAF No.39644
Posted from No.19 Sqn. Prewar RAF pilot with a SSC. First A Flight Commander from 12.07.40 to 12.12.40. Replaced by P.B.G. Davies when posted to

Z. SKARVADA

No.310 Sqn in July 1944 where he stayed until the end of war. Rapatriated to France after the war.
F/Sgt : 4-45

SLEPICA, Jaroslav   F/O   (cz)/RAF
7-44/8-45@   RAF No.186092

Posted from No.313 (Czech) Sqn. Arrived to the UK from internment in Soviet Union in October 1940. For short time posted to No.2 SS, in April 1941 posted to a pilot course. No.313 (Czech) Sqn July 1942 - August 1943. Second tour of operations with No.313 Sqn in March - July 1944. On 02.04.1948, he defected on board of a Spitfire from Czechoslovakia to Lüneburg located in the British Occupation Zone in Germany.

SMID, Borivoj   Sgt   (cz)/RAF
1-45/8-45@   RAF No.788527

Fresh graduate, posted from No.57 OTU. Volunteered for RAF service in 1942 as member of No.11 Cz Infantry Battalion in the Middle East. Remained with the new CzAF after 1945, but escaped to the UK on 24.03.50 as co-pilot of one of three Dakotas of Czechoslovak Airlines which flew to Germany. Rejoined RAF and served as an instructor pilot in No.1 Navigation School, being killed in a flying accident on 29.05.51 (Wellington T.10 RP382).
F/Sgt : 4-45

SMIK, Otto   P/O   (cz)/RAF
1-43/1-43, 3-44/7-44   RAF No.130578

Slovak born in Georgia (USSR). Prewar sport pilot. With Czech Depot at Agde 1940 then evacuated to the UK. Started pilot course in June 1941. Nos.312 (Czech) and 310 Sqns both in January 1943, then No.131 Sqn January - March 1943, No.122 Sqn March - May 1943, No.222 (Natal) Sqn May 1943 - October 1943 ending his tour of operations the same month. Second tour of operations with No.310 Sqn as Flying Officer posted from No.13 APC. Posted to No.312 Sqn becoming becoming B Flight commander

W. SNIECHOWSKI

A. STANEK

Czech and Polish pilot for strengthen of Czechoslovak-Polish co-operation.

SOKOL, Josef   Sgt   (CZ)/RAF
5-42/2-43, 8-43/8-45   RAF No.787523
     RAF No.149566
Posted from No.19 Sqn. Prewar pilot. With Czech Depot at Agde 1939-1940 then to GB. After retraining posted to No.19 Sqn in July 1941. Tour expired in February 1943. Second tour of operations with No.310 Sqn as Warrant Officer. Remained in CzAF after the war being killed on 17.07.46 in board of Spitfire TE572.
F/Sgt : 10-42, P-O : 9-43, F/O : 5-44

SOUKUP, Vladimir   F/Sgt   (CZ)/RAF
7-44/1-45   RAF No. 787409
Posted from No.312 (Czech) Sqn. With Czech Depot at Agde 1939-1940. Posted to No.312 (Czech) Sqn May 1943 - July 1944. Posted to Czech Depot.

SROM, Leopold   Sgt   (CZ)/RAF
7-41/8-42, 1-43/2-44   RAF No.787682
     RAF No.147011
See biography.
F/Sgt : 4-42, W/O : 1-43, P/O : 11-43

in July. On 03.09.44 he was shot but evaded capture returning to UK on 29.10.44. CO of No.127 Sqn November 1944 being killed a couple of days later. Eight confirmed and two confirmed shared victories and three flying bombs V-1s. DFC [No.222 Sqn].
†28.11.44, Spitfire XVI RR227, CO No.127 Sqn, Netherlands.

STANEK, Arnost   Sgt   (CZ)/RAF
12-41/9-42 (†)   RAF No.787158
Fresh graduate. Prewar pilot under training but started his pilot course in GB in August 1941 only.

SMOLKA, Erich   W/O   (CZ)/RAF
10-44/10-44   RAF No.787045
Posted from No.313 (Czech) Sqn. Prewar pilot. With Czech Depot at Agde in France in 1939-40 later to GB. No.313 (Czech) Sqn March 1943 - October 1944. Remained with No.310 Sqn one week only. Posted to No.312 (Czech) Sqn until the end of war. Later commissioned.

STEFAN, Benignus V.B.   F/O   (CZ)/RAF
6-42/6-42   RAF No.87624
Posted from No.57 OTU. In 1941 in Czechoslovak Depot. After four days only posted to No.313 (Czech) Sqn.
†08.03.43, Spitfire VB AR547, No.313 (Czech) Sqn, France.

SNIECHOWSKI, Wilhelm   P/O   PAF
6-41/12-41 (†)   RAF No.P0321
Posted from No.32 Sqn. Former prewar fighter pilot. He was evacuated to France via Romania where he served in a fighter defence flight in 1939-1940. On 20th June 1940 he was evacuated to Great Britain. Served with No.307 (Polish) Sqn September - October 1940, then No.32 Sqn February - June 1941. He was posted to No.310 Sqn as an exchange of one

STEFAN, Jan   F/Sgt   (CZ)/RAF
2-43/3-43   RAF No.787599
Posted from No.312 (Czech) Sqn. Prewar CzAF pilot. With FAF 1939-1940 serving in GC I/10 on Blochs then escaped to the UK. After retraining posted to No.1 Sqn October 1940 - July 1941, then No.65 Sqn

Leopold SROM
RAF No.787682 (NCO) & RAF No.147011 (Officer)

Born in Chrlice, near Brno, on 8th September 1917, Leopold Srom enlisted in the Army on 1st October 1937 after studying to be an electrician. He was posted to *Letecky pluk* 5 (Air Regiment 5) and passed the elementary flying training course. In May 1938 he started training as a fighter pilot, initially at *Letecky pluk* 4 at the Prague-Kbely airfield and subsequently at the Flying School at Prostejov. From December 1938 he served with the *Stihaci letka* 45 (Fighter Flight 45) of *Letecky pluk* 3 in Spisska Nova Ves. When, in March 1939, Czechoslovakia was divided into the Slovakian State and the Bohemia-Moravia Protektorat he returned home until 15th June when he escaped to Poland and then sailed to France. There, he joined the French Foreign Legion but when the war broke out he was posted for retraining to Oran - La Senia and Blida in Algeria. In November he returned to France and continued his training at Chartres, Bourges and La Rochelle. After the fall of France he escaped, from Bayonne, on 19th June 1940, to the United Kingdom. He joined the RAF, training on Battles at No.12 OTU and then on Hurricanes at No.56 OTU at Sutton Bridge. On 26th November, he was posted to his first operational unit with the rank of Sergeant. He served initially with No.245 Squadron in Northern Ireland and met his first enemy, in the air, on 10th May 1941. Together with Sergeant Vaclav Bauman he pursued a Bf110 without success. It is believed that this was the aircraft flown by the Nazi leader Rudolf Hess. Several days later, on 29th May, he claimed a Do17 as probably destroyed shared with Sergeant M. Hill. On 4th July he was posted to No.310 (Czechoslovak) Squadron, where he was subsequently able to make a number of claims Beginning on 12th July 1942, he claimed a Ju88 as destroyed and this was shared with Sergeant K.L. Pernica. On 23rd

July 1942 he returned from a *Rhubarb* mission with a *flak* damaged Spitfire. A *flak* battery around Lannion airfield had shot out a one meter section of the aircraft's starboard wing. On 1st August he was taken out of the line and sent for a rest as a flying instructor at No.57 OTU where he remained until 15th January 1943 when he returned to No.310 Squadron with the rank of Warrant Officer. On 31st January 1944 he was discharged from the RAF and subsequently obtained a posting to the Soviet Union to join the 1st Czechoslovak Fighter Regiment, where he flew La-5FN fighters over the Eastern Front. With the Slovakian Uprising in August it was decided to send the Regiment to support the insurgents and it arrived in central Slovakia on 17th September. Srom was one of the Regiment's most successful pilots during the fighting over Slovakia claiming three confirmed, one shared confirmed victory and two probables between 19th September and 18th October 1944, giving him an overall total of four confirmed, and two shared confirmed victories and two and one shared probable victories and two aircraft damaged. A week later the Regiment was withdrawn from Slovakia, and Srom was one of ten pilots who flew their aircraft back to Soviet territory. The remaining pilots withdrew to the mountains. On 16th January he was promoted to the rank of *porucik* (1st Lieutenant) and named leader of *2.letka* of *1.stihaci pluk*.

After the war he served for a short time with the CzAF but in autumn 1948 was at first arrested and then in the spring of 1949 Srom was dismissed from the service and began work as an electrician. In 1964 he was rehabilitated and promoted to the rank of Major. He joined CSA, the Czechoslovak airline and passed the examination to become a co-pilot, however he was killed in a flying accident at Prague-Ruzyne on 11th October 1968.

J.STIVAR

July 1941 - April 1942. Posted to No.313 (Czech) Sqn for a short time before returning to No.1 Sqn where he completed his first tour. Second tour of operations with No.312 (Czech) Sqn November 1942 - February 1943 before to be posted to No.310 Sqn. Posted to No.57 OTU in March 1943. No more operational posting until the end of war. After the Communist coup in 1948 he emigrated to UK, later moving to Canada.

STERBACEK, Jaroslav   P/O   (CZ)/RAF
7-40/8-40 (†)   RAF No.81901
Prewar CzAF bomber pilot with Air Regiment 5. With French Air Force 1939-1940 serving in ECD Chartres and Etampes.

STIBOR, Karel   Sgt   (CZ)/RAF
7-40/8-40   RAF No.787985

J.STRIHAVKA

Prewar pilot. With Czech Depot at Agde in France 1939-1940 then to the UK. Posted for retraining to No.6 OTU at Sutton Bridge.
†03.09.40, Hurricane I L1833, No.6 OTU, UK.

STIVAR, Josef   Sgt   (CZ)/RAF
4-42/7-43   RAF No.787512
Posted from No.57 OTU. Prewar pilot. With FAF 1939-1940 serving in Toulouse then to GB. After retraining posted in April 1942 to No.310 Sqn, his tour expiring in July 1943. Posted to No.2 DF. Second tour of operations with No.313 (Czech) Sqn October 1944 - May 1945.

STRIHAVKA, Jaromir   Sgt   (CZ)/RAF
10-40/8-41, 6-42/8-42, 2-43/7-44   RAF No.787657
       RAF No.115601
Posted from No.85 Sqn. Prewar CzAF fighter pilot in Air Regiment 3. With FAF 1939-1940 serving in Avord and Chartres before escaping to GB. After retraining posted in October 1940 shortly to No.85 Sqn. Posted to No.19 Sqn August 1941 - June 1942 before returning commissioned to No.310 Sqn to complete his first tour. Then served as an instructor. Second tour of operations February 1943 - July 1944, no more operational posting until the end of the war. For the return to Czechoslovakia in August 1945 he was posted to No.313 (Czech) Sqn. After the Communist coup in 1948 emigrated to the UK.
F/Sgt : 6-41, P/O : 6-42, F/O : 2-43

STUDENY, Jaroslav   P/O   (CZ)/RAF
7-40/11-40, 2-41/5-41   RAF No.82577
Prewar CzAF pilot. With Czech Depot at Agde 1939-1940 then to GB. Founder member of No.310 Sqn in July 1940, then CIG. In February 1941 he returned to No.310 Sqn, before to be posted to No.306 (Polish) Sqn as an exchange of one Czech and Polish pilot for strengthen of Czechoslovak-Polish co-operation in May 1941. There he stayed until July 1941 and then posted to various staff functions at Czechoslovak Inspectorate General till October 1944 when he moved to Soviet Union where he finished the war as an intelligence staff office of the 1st Cz Air Division.
F/O : 2-41

SVECENY, Antonin   Sgt   (CZ)/RAF
11-42/6-44   RAF No.787157

F. Trejtnar

Fresh graduate posted from No.53 OTU. Czech born in Ukraine. Prewar sport pilot. Attached to a group of Cz airmen in Agde in France 1939-1940. Posted for a pilot course in May 1941. Tour expired in June 1944 and posted to No.1 ADF.
F/Sgt : 11-43

SVOBODA, Jan   Sgt   (cz)/RAF
6-44/8-45@   RAF No.788154
Fresh graduate posted from No.84 GSU. Arrived to UK from internment in Soviet Union in June 1941. In February 1942 posted to pilot course.
W/O : 7-45

TAUBER, Pavel   Sgt   (CZ)/RAF
3-45/8-45@   RAF No.788536
Fresh graduate. Former member of the No.11 Cz Infantry Batallion in the Middle East before volunteer for the RAF.

TOCAUER, Stanislav   F/Sgt   (CZ)/RAF
11-43/2-44   RAF No.788044
Posted from No.1 ADF. Background unknown. No.1 AACU May - June 1941, then No. 9 SFTS and No.52 OTU. No.312 (Czech) Sqn February 1942 - May 1943.

Second tour of operations No.310 (Czech) Sqn from November 1943. Volunteered for Czechoslovak air unit on the Eastern Front in Soviet Union, and discharged RAF 31.01.44 sailing in February 1944. Became a founder member of 1st Cz Fighter Regiment and take a part in Slovak National Uprising. After repress of uprising he flew back to Soviet Union and he stayed 1st Cz Fighter Regiment after its reorganization till end of war.

TREJTNAR, Frantisek   Sgt   (CZ)/RAF
11-40/1-41, 5-41/6-42, 1-43/7-44   RAF No.787487
                                   RAF No.145002
Prewar CzAF fighter pilot in Air Regiment 3. With French Air Force 1939-1940 serving in Toulouse then to GB. After retraining posted to No.310 Sqn in November 1940. In January 1941 posted as test pilot to No.48 MU but returned to No.310 Sqn in May as Warrant Officer. Wounded in action on 23.06.1942 and withdrawn from operations until January 1943 when he was posted back to No.310 (Czech) Sqn and in July 1944 he left operational duty to be posted to Czechoslovak Depot till the end of war. For the return to Czechoslovakia in August 1945 he was posted to No.313 (Czech) Sqn. One cofirmed victory with No.310 Sqn, Europe, 1942.
F/Sgt : 6-41

VACULIK, Frantisek   F/Sgt   (CZ)/RAF
4-43/2-44   RAF No.787378
Posted from No.312 (Czech) Sqn. In the training at Flying School in Prostejov before the war. Attached to group of Cz airmen in Agde 1939-1940 before escaping to the UK. No.312 (Czech) Sqn April 1942 - April 1943. In February 1944, he volunteered for Czechoslovak air unit on the Eastern Front in Soviet Union (discharged RAF 31.01.44), becoming a founder member of 1st Cz Fighter Regiment and took part in Slovak National Uprising. He was shot down and killed by *flak* near Pravenec.
†20.09.44, La-5FN No.151, 1st Cz Fighter Regiment, Slovakia.

VALASEK, Pavel   F/Sgt   (CZ)/RAF
11-43/5-44   RAF No.787485
                                   RAF No.176089
Prewar sport pilot and under training at Flying School in Prostejov. With FAF 1939-1940 serving at Bordeaux, then to GB. Started pilot course in August 1941 only then No.313 (Czech) Sqn in December

F. VINDIS

1941 - May 1943. Tour expired May 1943. Second tour of operations with No.310 Sqn. Made PoW on 21.05.44 and liberated on 22.04.45.

VALOUSEK, Ladislav   Sgt   (CZ)/RAF
4-42/8-43   RAF No.787597
Posted from No.57 OTU. Prewar pilot. With FAF 1939-1940 serving in Toulouse then to the UK. Posted to pilot course in May 1941 and after completing his pilot course posted to No.310 Sqn in April 1942. Tour expired in August 1943 posted to No.2 ADF. Later volunteered for Czechoslovak air unit on the Eastern Front in Soviet Union sailing there in February 1944. Became the founder member of 1st Cz Fighter Regiment and took part in Slovak National Uprising. After repress of uprising he flew back to Soviet Union. Instructor with 2nd Cz Fighter Regiment from December 1944 onwards.
F/Sgt : 2-43

VINDIS, Frantisek   Sgt   (CZ)/RAF
10-40/12-42, 6-43/11-44   RAF No.787550
                             RAF No.158968
Prewar pilot. With FAF 1939-1940 serving with GC III/4 in Morocco then to GB. Tour expired December 1942, posted to No.10 FIS. Commissioned then second tour started with No.310 Sqn in June 1943 and

completed it in November 1944. Later served at CIG. For the return to Czechoslovakia in August 1945 he was posted to No.313 (Czech) Sqn. After the Communist coup in 1948 he emigrated to the UK and rejoined RAF. Two shared confirmed victories with No.310 Sqn, Europe 1944.
F/S : 4-42, W/O : 10-42

DFC : 08.01.45

VOPALECKY, Josef   Sgt   (CZ)/RAF
7-40/8-41   RAF No.787981
                             RAF No.102581
Prewar CzAF fighter pilot in Air Regiment 6. With FAF 1939-1940 serving with GCD I/55 then to GB. Posted to No.54 OTU for a night fighter course. Czech Flight No.68 Sqn February 42 - December 1943 then becoming staff officer of Czechoslovak Inspectorate General in London. Back to No.68 Sqn January - April 1945. After the war served with the new CzAF till 1950 when was fired out. Then he worked mainly as a truck driver. Two confirmed victories with No.68 Sqn, Europe 1944.
W/O : 6-41, P/O : 8-41

VYKOUKAL, Karel   P/O   (CZ)/RAF
7-40/8-40   RAF No.81902
Prewar CzAF fighter pilot in Air Regiment 4. With

J. VOPALECKY

FAF 1939-1940 serving in Chartres then to GB. Posted to No.6 OTU for retraining in August 1940 and in September 1940 posted to No.111 Sqn posted to No.73 Sqn the same month, then No.151 Sqn November - December 1940, No.17 Sqn December

1940 - May 1941, and No.313 (Czech) Sqn May 1941 - April 1942. Since March 1942 was leading B flight. No.41 Sqn April - May 1942 as flight leader.
† 21.05.42, Spitfire VB BL998, No.41 Sqn, France.

F. WEBER

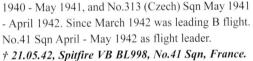

WEBER, Frantisek* P/O (CZ)/RAF
8-40/8-40, 1-41/1-42, 3-42/4-42 RAF No.82584
Prewar CzAF fighter pilot in Air Regiment 4. With Czech Depot at Agde 1939-1940 before escaping to the UK. Posted No.6 OTU for retraining in July 1940 and in September 1940 posted to No.145 Sqn, returning to No.310 Sqn as B flight CO on 01.01.41 replacing J. Jefferies. On 28.02.41 became Squadron CO, replaced by M.W.B. Knight at the head of B Flight. On 11.01.42 he collided with the Spitfire piloted by B. Kimlicka and spent two months in hospital. In April 1942 left squadron and became staff officer in Czechoslovak Inspectorate General in London. In 1943 he was sent for short term attachment to North Africa and Middle East. Between November 1943 and April 1944 he was the first CO of No.134 (Czech) Airfield (non-flying). Rest of war spent again in CIG. Remained with the new CzAF after 1945, but after communist coup in 1948 was arrested for two years in a Forced Labour Camp at Mirov.

S. ZIMPRICH

ZADROBILEK, Ladislav   P/O   (CZ)/RAF
11-42/1-43, 7-43/8-43   RAF No.132694
Posted from No.56 OTU. Prewar CzAF fighter pilot in Air Regiment 1. With FAF 1939-1940 serving in GC III/4 in Morocco then to GB. With No.111 Sqn November 1941 - May 1942 then completing his tour with No.313 (Czech) Sqn in May 1942 where he stayed for a short time. Second tour of operations with No.310 Sqn. On 02.01.43 seriously wounded in combat being back in July. Posted to 1943 ADF at Croydon. No more operational posting until the end of war. Remained with the new CzAF after 1945 but fired out in 1950, then working only in second-rate occupations.

ZAORAL, Vladimir   P/O   (CZ)/RAF
7-40/10-40, 10-40/11-41 (†)   RAF No.81903
Prewar CzAF fighter pilot in Air Regiment 2. With FAF 1939-1940 serving with ELD at Chartres, then to the UK. In October 1940 he was posted to No.501 Sqn for ten days only, claiming one confirmed victory with this unit.
F/O : 2-41

ZIMA, Rudolf   Sgt   (CZ)/RAF
7-40/3-41   RAF No.787978
With FAF 1939-1940 serving in EC Etampes and ELD Châteaudun, then to GB. Founder member of No. 310 Sqn in July 1940, then from March 1941 served as an instructor in EFTSes, later at EFTSes and SFTSes in Canada. After the war served with the new CzAF also as an instructor being fired out after communist coup in 1948.

ZIMPRICH, Stanislav   P/O   (CZ)/RAF
7-40/4-42 (†)   RAF No.81904
Prewar CzAF fighter pilot in Air Regiment 5. With FAF 1939-1940 serving with ELD Chartres and GC I/8 on Blochs before escaping to the UK. Founder member of No.310 Sqn in July 1940 and claimed one confirmed victory with No.310 Sqn, Battle of Britain, 1940.
F/O : 2-41, F/L : 2-42

ZOUHAR, Karel   P/O   (CZ)/RAF
11-42/4-44   RAF No.130858
Posted from No.57 OTU. Prewar pilot. With Czech Depot at Agde 1939-1940, then to GB. After retraining with No.6 OTU, posted to No.111 Sqn in November 1940. Tour of operations completed in April 1944. Second tour of operations with No.313 (Czech) Sqn September 1944 - May 1945.
F/O : 4-43

ZOUL, Stanislav   Sgt   (CZ)/RAF
3-45/8-45@   RAF No.788557
Fresh graduate. Member of No.11 Cz Infantry Battalion in the Middle East before volunteer for the RAF.

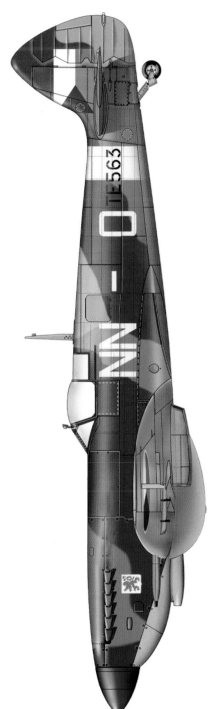

Supermarine Spitfire LF.IXE TE563, No.310 (Czechoslovak) Squadron, Manston, UK, August 1945.
This aircraft is wearing the Czech markings painted just before to make the way back to Prague. It is one of the 76
Spitfires the Czechoslovaks received before returning to their country.

SENIOR OFFICERS WHO FLEW WITH No.310
SQUADRON 1940-1945

BADER, Douglas R.S.   W/C   RAF
8-40/10-40   RAF No.26151
Prewar regular officer, being seriously injured in a
flying accident in December 1931, becoming invalid and could return to flying duty with the outbreak
of war, being posted to No.19 Sqn from November
1939. Then Flight Leader March - July 1940 with
No.222 (Natal) Squadron, then CO No.242
(Canadian) Sqn in July 1940. Became the forerun-
ner of the Wing concept during the Battle of Britain,
leading Squadrons into combat, organization which
was later officially formed. CO of Tangmere Wing
March 1941 until to be shot down on 09.08.41,
becoming a PoW. Twenty - four victories including
four shared, Dunkirk, Battle of Britain, Europe,
1940 -1941. DSO, DFC & BAR.

D.R.S.BADER & A.HESS

BITMEAD, Ernst R.   S/L   RAF
10-40/10-40   RAF No.34139
Prewar regular officer, with No.501 Sqn September
1939 - July 1940, then CO No.29 Sqn but before the
end of Battle of Britain, many attachments as supernumerary Squadron Leader with No.266 Sqn then
No.310 Sqn before taking command No.611
Squadron October 1940 - May 1941. Briefly in
charge of No.71 (Eagle) Sqn in August 1941 before being posted back for rest. No more operational
flying until the end of war. One confirmed victory,
DFC. Seven sorties with No.310 Sqn.

DOLEZAL, Frantisek   W/C   (CZ)/RAF
3-43/2-44   RAF No.82593
See biography in Squadron pilot roster. Flew with
No.310 Squadron as Wing Commander of the
Czechoslovakian Wing/No.134 Wing between April
1943 - February 1944. Second Czech fighter to be
awarded the DSO.

HLADO, Jaroslav   W/C   (CZ)/RAF
12-44/8-45   RAF No.125414
Prewar CzAF fighter pilot in Air Regiment 1 & 4,
former member of Czechoslovak competition team
before the war (Zürich 1937), then test pilot of Avia
aircraft factory. Escaped to Ukraine in August 1940
with a Avia B-534, but was put into jail until 1941.
Liberated and arrived in the UK in Spring 1942.
With No.131 Sqn January - February 1943, No.122
Sqn February - May 1943, then No.222 (Natal) Sqn
May - November 1943. Second tour of operation
duty with No.312 (Czech) Sqn April - November
1944, leading the unit from mid-May 1944 until
taking command of No.134 (Czech) Wing in
December. Last Czech fighter pilot to be awarded
the DSO.

J.HLADO

MRAZEK, Karel   W/C   (CZ)/RAF
6-42/3-43   RAF No. 82561
See biography in Squadron pilot roster. Flew with
No.310 Squadron as Exeter Wing leader. First
Czech fighter pilot to be awarded the DSO.

VASATKO, Alois   W/C   (CZ)/RAF
5-42/6-42   RAF No.83233
Known as "*Amos*". Prewar CzAF reconnaissance
pilot with Air Regiment 2. Served with the French

Wing Commander Jaroslav HLADO, D.F.C. (125414), Royal Air Force, No.134 (Czechoslovak) Wing.

Since taking over leadership of the Czech Wing, Wing Commander Hlado has shown a determination and offensive spirit of the highest order. His work has been all the more difficult in that during their task of escorting bombers on day-light missions, neither the escort nor their charges were touched by the enemy. The fact that their presence alone deterred the enemy from attacking the bomber stream was poor consolation to the Fighter pilots concerned and the Wing Leader´s efforts and abilities in attaining an aggresive spirit were taxed to the utmost. Nevertheless, by sheer force of character, example and determination, he achieved that spirit, and as a result of his efforts, all bombers under the care of the Czech Wing, were kept free from molestation.

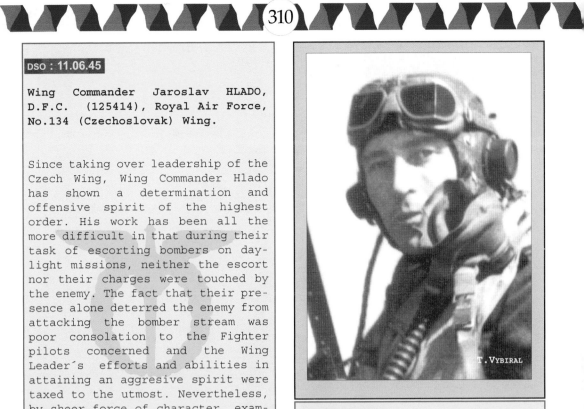

T. VYBIRAL

Wing Commander Tomas VYBIRAL, D.F.C. (83236), Royal Air Force, No.134 (Czechoslovak) Wing.
Originally recommended to DFC & Bar, but on 28.12.1944 awarded DSO by Air Marshal Roderic Hill.

This very gallant Czechoslovakian Officer has been flying operationally since he has driven from his own country to France in 1939 and has flown 650 hours in operations against the enemy.
Since January 1944 he has led his Country´s Wing with the Royal Air Force and during this time has carried out many missions escorting bombers and ground straffing, particulary during the intensive period of the invasion of Normandy.
Although faced with many difficulties in commanding a Wing for which replacements are scarce, Wing Commander Vybiral has maintained a high pitch of efficiency and enthusiasm among his pilots and has shown a personel example that is beyond praise.

with GC I/5 on Curtisses becoming the second of the top scorers of the French Air Force in 1939-1940. Then escaped to the UK and became the first CO of No.312 (Czech) Squadron September 1940 - May 1942. Then promoted to command Exeter wing. Killed colliding with a FW190 while flying with No.310 Squadron. Four confirmed victories (three with the French) and eleven shared destroyed (nine with the French), 1940 - 1941. DFC.
†23.06.42, *Spitfire VB BM592, CO Exeter Wing, UK.*

VYBIRAL, Tomas   W/C   (CZ)/RAF
2-44/11-44   RAF No.83236
Prewar CzAF pilot with Air Regiment 4. After the German occupation, he reached France via Poland. With French Air Force 1939-1940 serving with GC I/5 on Curtisses, then to GB. Founder member of No.312 (Czech) Sqn September 1940 - August 1942, then CO November 1942 - November 1943. Third Czech fighter pilot to be awarded the DSO.

© www.venturapublications.com

Supermarine Spitfire Mk.IXC MK483, Wing Commander Tomas Vybiral, No.134 (Czechoslovak) Wing, Appledram, June 1944.